The Rhubarb Cookbook
Delightful Recipes for Sweet and Tangy Treats

De Oyster Paradise

Copyright © 2023 De Oyster Paradise
All rights reserved.
:

Contents

INTRODUCTION 7
1. Rhubarb Crumble 9
2. Rhubarb Pie 9
3. Rhubarb Compote 10
4. Rhubarb Sauce 11
5. Rhubarb Jam 12
6. Rhubarb Tart 13
7. Rhubarb Sorbet 13
8. Rhubarb Ice Cream 14
9. Rhubarb Muffins 15
10. Rhubarb Bread 16
11. Rhubarb Scones 17
12. Rhubarb Cookies 18
13. Rhubarb Brownies 19
14. Rhubarb Cake 20
15. Rhubarb Cheesecake 21
16. Rhubarb Pudding 22
17. Rhubarb Custard 23
18. Rhubarb Trifle 24
19. Rhubarb Smoothie 25
20. Rhubarb Juice 26
21. Rhubarb Cocktail 26
22. Rhubarb Lemonade 27
23. Rhubarb Punch 28
24. Rhubarb Mojito 28
25. Rhubarb Margarita 29
26. Rhubarb Sangria 30
27. Rhubarb Spritzer 31

28. Rhubarb Tea 32
29. Rhubarb Coffee 32
30. Rhubarb Hot Chocolate 33
31. Rhubarb Pancakes 34
32. Rhubarb Waffles 35
33. Rhubarb French Toast 36
34. Rhubarb Omelette 37
35. Rhubarb Quiche 38
36. Rhubarb Frittata 39
37. Rhubarb Stir Fry 40
38. Rhubarb Curry 41
39. Rhubarb Soup 42
40. Rhubarb Stew 43
41. Rhubarb Chili 43
42. Rhubarb Marinade 44
43. Rhubarb Gravy 45
44. Rhubarb Dressing 46
45. Rhubarb Stuffing 47
46. Rhubarb Roast 48
47. Rhubarb Ribs 49
48. Rhubarb Chicken 50
49. Rhubarb Beef 51
50. Rhubarb Pork 52
51. Rhubarb Lamb 53
52. Rhubarb Duck 54
53. Rhubarb Fish 55
54. Rhubarb Shrimp 56
55. Rhubarb Crab 57
56. Rhubarb Salad 57

57. Rhubarb Coleslaw 58
58. Rhubarb Potato Salad 59
59. Rhubarb Pasta Salad 60
60. Rhubarb Quinoa Salad 60
61. Rhubarb Rice Salad 61
62. Rhubarb Bean Salad 62
63. Rhubarb Egg Salad 63
64. Rhubarb Chicken Salad 64
65. Rhubarb Tuna Salad 65
66. Rhubarb Fruit Salad 66
67. Rhubarb Cheese Ball 66
68. Rhubarb Guacamole 67
69. Rhubarb Hummus 68
70. Rhubarb Pesto 69
71. Rhubarb Dip 70
72. Rhubarb Tapenade 71
73. Rhubarb Bruschetta 71
74. Rhubarb Crostini 72
75. Rhubarb Pizza 73
76. Rhubarb Quesadilla 74
77. Rhubarb Burrito 75
78. Rhubarb Enchilada 76
79. Rhubarb Taco 77
80. Rhubarb Burger 78
81. Rhubarb Hot Dog 79
82. Rhubarb Sandwich 80
83. Rhubarb Wrap 81
84. Rhubarb Panini 81
85. Rhubarb Grilled Cheese 82

86. Rhubarb Focaccia 83
87. Rhubarb Bagel 84
88. Rhubarb English Muffin 85
89. Rhubarb Biscuit 86
90. Rhubarb Croissant 87
91. Rhubarb Danish 88
92. Rhubarb Turnover 89
93. Rhubarb Empanada 90
94. Rhubarb Samosa 91
95. Rhubarb Dumpling 92
96. Rhubarb Pierogi 93
97. Rhubarb Gnocchi 94
98. Rhubarb Lasagna 95
99. Rhubarb Shepherd's Pie 96
100. Rhubarb Moussaka 97
101. Rhubarb Biryani 98
102. Rhubarb Paella 99
103. Rhubarb Sushi 100
104. Rhubarb Spring Rolls 101
CONCLUSION 103

INTRODUCTION

Introduction for The Rhubarb Cookbook: 104 Delightful Recipes for Sweet and Tangy Treats

Rhubarb, the sweet and tangy savory that leaves lasting flavour in the mouth, is growing in popularity amongst the top chefs and foodies all around the world. From cakes, pies and crumbles to jams, jellies and even liqueurs, rhubarb's versatile properties make it suitable for a wide range of dishes that not only tantalize the taste buds but also bring bright hues of pink and red to the table.

The Rhubarb Cookbook: 104 Delightful Recipes for Sweet and Tangy Treats is a comprehensive collection of recipes tailored to the needs of both novice cooks and experienced rhubarb cravers. Inside these pages, you'll find an exquisite selection of traditional favourites as well as inventive and unusual recipes just waiting to be explored. From sweet and savouring rhubarb desserts and preserves to the delightful flavour possibilities of soup, juice and even meat dishes, this book truly does capture the diversity of cooking with rhubarb.

The Rhubarb Cookbook features easy-to-follow recipes that make for an effortless - yet exquisite - cooking experience. Regardless of enthusiasm and level of kitchen skills, each recipe is designed to help you explore the full potential of rhubarb without breaking the bank. Expect traditional baking favourites such as rhubarb-strawberry crumbles, warm rhubarb puddings and vibrant pink jams, as well as more innovative dishes including rhubarb vinaigrette, rhubarb chutney and baked rhubarb macaroni and cheese.

Along with the delicious recipes, The Rhubarb Cookbook also contains a section dedicated to rhubarb growing tips, from planting and tending to the plant to harvesting and storing the stalks. Not to mention, the book even provides a comprehensive guide to selecting and preparing rhubarb for the perfect cooking experience.

So no matter if you're a beginner in rhubarb cooking or an experienced baker, The Rhubarb Cookbook is sure to become a go-to for anyone looking to explore the full flavour potential of this unique vegetable. Step into the world of rhubarb cooking and create a culinary masterpiece with this amazing guide. Bon appetite!

1. Rhubarb Crumble

This Rhubarb Crumble is a delicious and easy-to-make dessert that combines sweet and tart rhubarb with a buttery crumble topping.
Serving: 8
Preparation time: 10 minutes
Ready time: 30 minutes

Ingredients:
- 4 cups of chopped rhubarb
- 3/4 cup granulated sugar
- 2 tablespoons all-purpose flour
- 2 tablespoons cornstarch
- 1/2 cup cold unsalted butter, cubed
- 1 cup all-purpose flour
- 1/2 cup packed brown sugar
- 1 teaspoon ground cinnamon

Instructions:
1. Preheat oven to 350F. Grease 8-inch baking dish with butter.
2. In a bowl, combine rhubarb, granulated sugar, 2 tablespoons flour and cornstarch. Pour mixture into baking dish.
3. In a medium bowl, combine butter, 1 cup of flour, brown sugar and cinnamon. Cut butter into flour mixture until it resembles coarse crumbs. Sprinkle topping mixture over rhubarb.
4. Bake in preheated oven for 30 minutes or until golden and bubbling. Let cool before serving.

Nutrition information: Calories: 234; Total Fat: 11.2g; Saturated Fat: 7g; Cholesterol: 30mg; Sodium: 49mg; Carbohydrates: 33.1g; Protein:1.9g; Fiber: 1.5g; Sugar: 19.3g.

2. Rhubarb Pie

Rhubarb Pie is a classic dessert that pairs sweet and tart flavors in a timeless way. It features a flaky pastry crust with a sweet-tart baked rhubarb filling.

Serving
This recipe will serve 8 people.
Preparation Time
This recipe takes 25 minutes to prepare.
Ready time
The cooking time for this recipe takes 45 minutes.

Ingredients:
- 2¼ cups all-purpose flour
- 1 teaspoon salt
- 1 cup vegetable shortening
- 7-8 tablespoons cold water
- 3 cups diced rhubarb
- 1 cup sugar
- 3 tablespoons cornstarch
- 1 teaspoon ground ginger
- 1/4 teaspoon ground nutmeg

Instructions:
1. Preheat oven to 375 degrees.
2. In a large bowl, combine the flour and salt. Cut in the shortening and mix until it resembles coarse crumbs. Sprinkle the water over the mixture, stirring with a fork until it looks like coarse crumbs. Form into a ball.
3. On a lightly floured surface, roll out the pastry and transfer to a 9-inch pie pan.
4. In a medium bowl, combine the rhubarb, sugar, cornstarch, ginger and nutmeg. Stir until evenly blended. Pour the mixture into the pie crust.
5. Bake for 45 minutes, or until the crust is golden brown and the filling is bubbling.
6. Let cool for at least 1 hour before serving.

Nutrition information
Calories: 317; Fat: 13.6g; Saturated Fat: 5.9g; Cholesterol: 11mg; Sodium: 295mg; Carbohydrates: 45.6g; Fiber: 2.2g; Sugars: 16.9g; Protein: 3.5g.

3. Rhubarb Compote

Rhubarb compote is a delicious fruit-based side dish that can be served warm or cold. Boasting a tart flavor, this easy-to-make treat is a great way to add a little somethin' somethin' to breakfast, lunch, or even dinner.
Serving: 4
Preparation time: 10 minutes
Ready time: 20 minutes

Ingredients:
- 4 large stalks of rhubarb, washed and cut into 1/2-inch pieces
- 2/3 cup granulated sugar
- 2 tablespoons fresh lemon juice
- 1 teaspoon ground cinnamon
- 2 tablespoons water

Instructions:
1. In a medium sized saucepan, combine the rhubarb, sugar, lemon juice, cinnamon, and water. Bring to a boil over medium-high heat, stirring frequently.
2. Once boiling, reduce the heat to low and simmer for 10 minutes, or until the rhubarb is soft and the liquid has thickened.
3. Remove from the heat and let cool. Serve warm or cold.

Nutrition information: per serving of rhubarb compote (1/4 of a batch):
Calories: 119, Total fat: 0g, Saturated fat: 0g, Cholesterol: 0mg, Sodium: 0mg, Carbohydrates: 29g, Fiber: 3g, Sugars: 23g, Protein: 1g.

4. Rhubarb Sauce

Rhubarb Sauce is a delicious and sweet-tart condiment made from cooked rhubarb. The finished sauce is perfect for topping cakes, cookies, and other desserts, or served with ice cream.
Serving: Makes about 4-5 servings
Preparation time: 10 minutes
Ready time: 40 minutes

Ingredients:
* 8 cups rhubarb, diced

* 2 cups white sugar
* ½ teaspoon ground cinnamon
* ¼ teaspoon ground nutmeg

Instructions:
1. In a large saucepan, combine rhubarb, sugar, cinnamon, and nutmeg.
2. Bring mixture to a boil over medium-high heat.
3. Reduce heat to medium-low and simmer uncovered for 25 minutes, stirring occasionally.
4. Remove from heat and let cool.
5. Refrigerate until ready to serve.

Nutrition information: Per Serving: Calories 228, Carbohydrates 57g, Protein 1g, Total Fat 0g, Sodium 15mg, Fiber 3g

5. Rhubarb Jam

Rhubarb Jam is a tart and sweet jam made from fresh rhubarb, perfect for spreading on your favorite toast or pastries!
Serving: Makes 2 8-ounce jars.
Preparation Time: 10 minutes
Ready Time: Approx. 45 minutes

Ingredients:
- 1 lb fresh rhubarb, diced
- 2/3 cup white sugar
- 2 tablespoons lemon juice

Instructions:
1. In a large saucepan, combine diced rhubarb, sugar and lemon juice.
2. Heat over medium heat, stirring frequently, until mixture comes to a bubble.
3. Reduce heat and simmer for 20-25 minutes until rhubarb is broken down and mixture thickens.
4. Remove from heat and spoon jam into 8-ounce jars.
5. Allow to cool and store in refrigerator.

Nutrition information: Serving Size: 1 tablespoon (60ml), Calories: 22, Total Fat: 0g, Sodium: 0mg, Potassium: 24mg, Total Carbs: 5g, Sugars: 5g, Protein: 0g.

6. Rhubarb Tart

Rhubarb Tart is a delicious, sweet and tangy dessert that combines the flavor of fresh rhubarb and a buttery crust.
Serving: Makes 8 to 10 servings
Preparation time: 10 minutes
Ready time: 45 minutes

Ingredients:
- 3/4 cup sugar
- 2 tablespoons cornstarch
- ¼ teaspoon kosher salt
- 2½ pounds rhubarb, cut into 1/2-inch pieces
- 2 tablespoons unsalted butter
- 9-inch prepared tart shell

Instructions:
1. In a large bowl, whisk together sugar, cornstarch and salt.
2. Add the rhubarb and toss to thoroughly coat it.
3. Heat the butter in a large skillet over medium-high heat.
4. Add the rhubarb and cook until it starts to soften, about 5 minutes.
5. Spread the filled rhubarb evenly in the tart shell.
6. Bake for 25 to 30 minutes, until the rhubarb is cooked through and the crust is golden.

Nutrition information: Serving size - 1 slice. Calories - 240, Total fat - 5 grams, Cholesterol - 15 milligrams, Sodium - 120 milligrams, Total carbohydrate - 45 grams, Protein - 3 grams.

7. Rhubarb Sorbet

Rhubarb Sorbet is an easy and refreshing dessert recipe that combines tart rhubarb with a hint of orange zest and a light touch of sugar. This sweet and creamy sorbet is perfect for hot summer days.
Serving: Makes 12 servings
Preparation Time: 10 minutes
Ready Time: 4 hours

Ingredients:
- 4 cups rhubarb, trimmed and cut into 1/2-inch pieces
- 1/2 cup granulated sugar
- 1/2 cup water
- 1/2 teaspoon freshly grated orange zest

Instructions:
1. Place the rhubarb, sugar, and water in a large saucepan, and bring to a boil over medium heat. Reduce the heat to low, and simmer for 15 minutes.
2. Remove the pan from the heat, and stir in the orange zest. Allow the mixture to cool to room temperature.
3. Place the cooled rhubarb mixture in a blender, and purée until smooth. Pass the purée through a sieve to remove any lumps.
4. Pour the purée into a shallow container, and freeze for 1-2 hours.
5. Remove the container from the freezer, and stir with a fork to break up any large pieces. Freeze again for 1 hour.
6. Stir the sorbet again with a fork, breaking up any clumps that may have formed. Freeze for 2 hours, or until firm.

Nutrition information: per serving (1/12 of recipe): 119 calories; 1.5 g fat; 0.3 g saturated fat; 27.5 g carbohydrates; 1.2 g protein; 1.8 g fiber.

8. Rhubarb Ice Cream

Rhubarb Ice Cream is an easy and delicious dessert that is perfect for all occasions. This delicious ice cream is made with fresh rhubarb, cream, and sugar.
Serving: 8-10
Preparation time: 10 minutes

Ready time: 10 minutes

Ingredients:
- 2 cups fresh rhubarb, finely chopped
- 1/2 cup white granulated sugar
- 1 cup heavy cream
- 1 teaspoon vanilla extract

Instructions:
1. Place the rhubarb in a medium-sized saucepan. Add the sugar and stir to combine.
2. Bring the mixture to a boil over medium-high heat, stirring frequently.
3. Reduce the heat and simmer for 5 minutes, stirring occasionally.
4. Transfer the mixture to a medium bowl and allow it to cool.
5. Once the mixture has cooled, add the heavy cream and vanilla extract. Stir until combined.
6. Transfer the mixture to an ice cream maker and follow the instructions on the machine.
7. Once the ice cream is ready, scoop it into serving dishes and enjoy immediately.

Nutrition information: Serving size: 1/2 cup; Calories: 200; Total fat: 11 g; Saturated fat: 7 g; Sodium: 20 mg; Total carbohydrate: 23 g; Dietary fiber: 2 g; Sugars: 18 g; Protein: 2 g.

9. Rhubarb Muffins

These delicious Rhubarb Muffins are bursting with flavor and make a perfect afternoon treat.
Serving: Makes 12 muffins
Preparation time: 10 minutes
Ready time: 35 minutes

Ingredients:
- 2 cups all-purpose flour
- ¾ cup sugar
- 2 teaspoons baking powder
- ½ teaspoon baking soda

- ½ teaspoon salt
- 1 egg
- 1 cup plain Greek yogurt
- 2 tablespoons vegetable oil
- 1 teaspoon vanilla extract
- 1 cup chopped fresh or frozen rhubarb
- 2 tablespoons sugar
- 1 teaspoon ground cinnamon

Instructions:
1. Preheat the oven to 400 degrees F. Grease a 12-cup muffin pan with nonstick cooking spray.
2. In a large bowl, whisk together the flour, sugar, baking powder, baking soda, and salt.
3. In a separate bowl, whisk together the egg, yogurt, oil, and vanilla extract. Stir the wet Ingredients into the dry Ingredients until just combined.
4. In a small bowl, combine the rhubarb, sugar, and cinnamon. Fold the rhubarb mixture into the muffin batter.
5. Divide the batter evenly among the muffin cups. Bake for 18-20 minutes, or until a toothpick inserted into the center of a muffin comes out clean.
6. Let cool in the pan for 5 minutes before transferring to a wire rack to cool completely.

Nutrition information:
Serving size: 1 muffin
Calories: 200
Fat: 4.5 g
Carbs: 36 g
Protein: 5 g

10. Rhubarb Bread

Rhubarb Bread is an easy-to-make and delicious quick bread, with unique tart flavour from the rhubarb.
Serving: Makes about 8-10 servings.
Preparation Time: 15 minutes

Ready Time: 50 minutes

Ingredients:
- 2 cups all-purpose flour
- 1 teaspoon baking soda
- 2 teaspoons baking powder
- 1/2 teaspoon salt
- 2 large eggs
- 1 teaspoon vanilla extract
- 1/2 cup vegetable oil
- 1/2 cup white sugar
- 1/2 cup light brown sugar
- 1/4 cup milk
- 2 1/2 cups fresh, diced rhubarb

Instructions:
1. Preheat the oven to 350 degrees F (175 degrees C).
2. Grease an 8x4 inch loaf pan.
3. Combine the flour, baking soda, baking powder, and salt in a bowl.
4. In a separate bowl, beat together the eggs, vanilla extract, oil, white sugar and brown sugar.
5. Slowly mix in the dry Ingredients.
6. Stir in the milk and the diced rhubarb.
7. Pour the mixture into the prepared loaf pan.
8. Bake for 45 to 50 minutes, or until a toothpick inserted in the center comes out clean.

Nutrition information: Serving size: 1 piece (1/8 of loaf); Calories: 241; Fat: 9g; Carbs: 39g; Protein: 3g

11. Rhubarb Scones

Enjoy a delicious and easy-to-make snack with these Rhubarb Scones. They pair great with a cup of tea or coffee and will be a hit with the entire family.
Serving: 8 Scones
Preparation Time: 10 Minutes
Ready Time: 25 Minutes

Ingredients:
- 2 cups all-purpose flour
- 2 teaspoons baking powder
- 1/2 teaspoon salt
- 1/3 cup granulated sugar
- 1/2 cup cold butter, cubed
- 3/4 cup diced rhubarb
- 1/2 cup cold heavy cream
- 2 teaspoons vanilla extract

Instructions:
1. Preheat oven to 425°F.
2. In a medium bowl, combine flour, baking powder, salt and sugar.
3. Cut in butter using a pastry cutter or fork until the butter is in small pieces.
4. Add rhubarb and stir to coat.
5. In a separate bowl, whisk together cream and vanilla extract.
6. Add cream mixture to the flour mixture, stirring until just combined.
7. Turn dough out on a lightly floured surface. Knead dough gently a few times just until it comes together.
8. Roll dough into an 8-inch circle and cut into 8 wedges.
9. Place scones on a baking sheet lined with parchment paper.
10. Bake for 18-22 minutes, or until golden brown.
11. Remove from oven and let cool before serving.

Nutrition information: Per scone: 155 calories, 9.5g fat, 17g carbohydrates, 1.3g fiber, 5.3g protein.

12. Rhubarb Cookies

These rhubarb cookies are a delicious, crisp-on-the-outside, chewy-on-the inside treat! They make a great snack or addition to any meal.
Serving: 24 cookies
Preparation Time: 30 minutes
Ready Time: 1 hour

Ingredients:

- 2 cups all-purpose flour
- 1 teaspoon baking powder
- ½ teaspoon baking soda
- ¼ teaspoon salt
- ½ cup butter, softened
- ½ cup white sugar
- ½ cup packed light brown sugar
- 1 egg
- 1 teaspoon vanilla extract
- 1 ½ cups finely chopped rhubarb

Instructions:
1. Preheat oven to 375 degrees F (190 degrees C).
2. In a medium bowl, whisk together flour, baking powder, baking soda and salt.
3. In a large bowl, cream together butter, white sugar and brown sugar until light and fluffy. Beat in egg and vanilla.
4. Gradually mix in flour mixture into the butter mixture. Stir in rhubarb.
5. Drop dough by teaspoonfuls onto a ungreased baking sheet.
6. Bake for 10 to 12 minutes in the preheated oven, until golden brown.
7. Allow cookies to cool for 1 minute on the baking sheet before transferring to a wire rack to cool completely.

Nutrition information: Per serving (1 cookie): 75 calories; 25 calories from fat; 3 g of fat; 2 g of saturated fat; 15 mg of cholesterol; 50 mg of sodium; 12 g of carbohydrates; 1 g of dietary fiber; 5 g of sugar; and 1 g of protein.

13. Rhubarb Brownies

Deliciously indulgent rhubarb brownies, the perfect dessert for any occasion.
Serving: Makes 12 brownies
Preparation time: 15 minutes
Ready time: 45 minutes

Ingredients:
- 150g soft butter

- 150g light brown sugar
- 3 eggs
- 1 teaspoon vanilla extract
- 125g self-raising flour
- 100g cocoa powder
- 150g rhubarb, chopped
- 1 tablespoon demerara sugar

Instructions:
1. Preheat oven to 200c/180c fan/gas 6. Grease and line a 20cm square tin.
2. Cream together the butter and sugar until pale and creamy.
3. Beat in the eggs one at a time and add the vanilla extract.
4. Sieve together the flour and cocoa powder and fold into the mixture with a metal spoon.
5. Stir in the chopped rhubarb and spoon the mixture into the prepared tin.
6. Sprinkle the top with demerara sugar and bake for 40 minutes until risen and a skewer comes out clean when inserted into the middle of the brownies.
7. Leave to cool for 10 minutes before cutting into 12 even squares.

Nutrition information:
Calories: 208kcal, Protein: 3.4g, Carbs: 22.7g, Fat: 11.1g, Fibre: 1.2g

14. Rhubarb Cake

This Rhubarb Cake is a delicious and sweet treat for any occasion. The tartness of the rhubarb pairs perfectly with the sweetness of the cake.
Serving: 8
Preparation Time: 30 minutes
Ready Time: 1 hour

Ingredients:
- 2 cups all-purpose flour
- 1 teaspoon baking powder
- 1 teaspoon baking soda
- 1/2 teaspoon salt

- 1 cup butter, softened
- 2 cups white sugar
- 2 eggs
- 3/4 cup milk
- 1 teaspoon vanilla extract
- 3 cups chopped fresh rhubarb

Instructions:
1. Preheat oven to 350 degrees F (175 degrees C). Grease and flour a 9x13 inch pan.
2. In a medium bowl, stir together the flour, baking powder, baking soda, and salt.
3. In a large bowl, cream together the butter and sugar until smooth. Beat in the eggs one at a time, then stir in the milk and vanilla. Gradually stir the dry Ingredients into the batter just until blended. Fold in the rhubarb. Spread into the prepared pan.
4. Bake for 40 to 50 minutes in the preheated oven, until a toothpick inserted into the center of the cake comes out clean.

Nutrition information:
Serving Size: 8
Calories: 320
Total Fat: 13g
Cholesterol: 48mg
Sodium: 229mg
Total Carbohydrates: 44g
Dietary Fiber: 1.3g
Sugar: 25g
Protein: 3.6g

15. Rhubarb Cheesecake

This Rhubarb Cheesecake recipe takes a classic dessert up a notch with the tartness of rhubarb baked in a delicious shortbread base.
Serving: Serves 8
Preparation time: 15 minutes
Ready time: 1 hour and 45 minutes

Ingredients:
- 3 tablespoons butter, plus extra for greasing
- 2 cups ground shortbread
- 4 eggs
- 400g tub ricotta cheese
- 8 ounces cream cheese, softened
- 2/3 cup granulated sugar
- 1 teaspoon vanilla extract
- 14 ounces frozen rhubarb
- 6 tablespoons golden caster sugar

Instructions:
1. Preheat the oven to 350°F (175°C) and grease a 9-inch round cake tin with butter.
2. In a bowl, combine the ground shortbread and melted butter and mix until combined. Press the mixture into the bottom of the greased cake tin.
3. In another bowl, whisk together the eggs, ricotta, cream cheese, granulated sugar, and vanilla extract. Pour the mixture into the cake tin and spread evenly.
4. In a separate bowl, combine the frozen rhubarb and golden caster sugar. Spoon the rhubarb mixture into the cake tin and spread evenly on top of the cheese mixture.
5. Bake in the preheated oven for 1 hour and 45 minutes or until golden brown.

Nutrition information: Per serving: 335 calories; 18.6g fat; 35.5g carbohydrates; 5.1g protein

16. Rhubarb Pudding

Rhubarb Pudding is a tangy twist to a classic pudding. Combining the tartness of rhubarb with creamy custard makes for a delightful dessert.
Serving: 8
Preparation Time: 15 minutes
Ready Time: 1 hour and 15 minutes

Ingredients:

- 2½ cups peeled and chopped rhubarb
- 1 cup white sugar
- 2 tablespoons all-purpose flour
- 2 tablespoons butter
- 1 cup milk
- 1/2 cup heavy cream
- 1 teaspoon ground nutmeg
- 2 eggs

Instructions:
1. Preheat oven to 350 degrees F (175 degrees C).
2. Place rhubarb, sugar, flour, and butter in a 9x9 inch baking dish. Stir together until evenly blended.
3. In a medium bowl, whisk together the milk, cream, nutmeg, and eggs. Pour over rhubarb mixture.
4. Bake in preheated oven for 45 minutes, or until a toothpick inserted into center of pudding comes out clean.

Nutrition information: Calories: 244, Fat: 9g, Saturated Fat: 5g, Cholesterol: 67mg, Sodium: 54mg, Potassium: 150mg, Carbohydrates: 36g, Fiber: 1g, Sugar: 27g, Protein: 4g.

17. Rhubarb Custard

Rhubarb Custard is a favorite British pudding that is made of Stewed Rhubarb and Egg Custard.
Serving: 4
Preparation Time: 15 minutes
Ready Time: 45 minutes

Ingredients:
- 500g rhubarb, trimmed and chopped
- 3 tablespoons caster sugar
- 2 large eggs
- 300ml single cream
- 3 tablespoons caster sugar
- Splash of vanilla extract

Instructions:
1. Preheat the oven to 180C/Gas mark 4.
2. Place the rhubarb in an oven proof dish, sprinkle the 3 tablespoons of caster sugar over the rhubarb and bake for 20-25 minutes.
3. In a large bowl whisk together the eggs and cream.
4. Add the remaining sugar and a splash of vanilla extract and whisk together. Gently fold in the rhubarb.
5. Pour the mixture into an oven proof dish and bake for 30-35 minutes.
6. Serve warm with a dollop of cream on top.

Nutrition information: (approx. per serving)
Calories: 277 | Fat: 14.6g | Carbs: 25.8g | Protein: 6.9g

18. Rhubarb Trifle

This Rhubarb Trifle is a classic British pudding made with layers of crispy custard-soaked sponge fingers, layered with stewed rhubarb and delicious creamy custard. Additionally, it is topped off with a sprinkle of mixed nut crumble.
Serving: 6-8
Preparation time: 10 minutes
Ready time: 40 minutes

Ingredients:
- 8 ounces (230 grams) thinly sliced fresh rhubarb
- 4 ounces (110 grams) caster sugar
- 2 tablespoons (30 milliliters) lemon juice
- 1 teaspoon (5 milliliters) ground ginger
- 3 tablespoons (45 grams) unsalted butter
- 4 ounces (110 grams) sponge finger biscuits
- 1 pint (500 milliliters) double cream
- 2 egg yolks
- 2 ounces (60 grams) demerara sugar
- 2 ounces (60 grams) chopped mixed nuts

Instructions:
1. Preheat your oven to 350°F (180°C).

2. Put the rhubarb, caster sugar, lemon juice, ginger and butter into a baking dish and cook in the oven for 20 minutes or until the rhubarb has softened.
3. Place the sponge fingers in the base of a large bowl.
4. Pour the rhubarb mixture over the top of the sponge fingers.
5. In a separate bowl, beat the cream until it forms soft peaks.
6. In a separate bowl, beat the egg yolks and demerara sugar until pale and creamy.
7. Gently fold the cream into the egg mixture.
8. Pour the custard over the rhubarb mixture in the bowl.
9. Sprinkle the chopped mixed nuts over the top of the trifle.
10. Place in the fridge to set for at least 20 minutes.

Nutrition information: Calories: 266; Fat: 16.6g; Cholesterol: 57mg; Sodium: 25.5mg; Carbohydrates: 28.6g; Fiber: 1.3g; Protein: 3.8g.

19. Rhubarb Smoothie

Start every day refreshed with this delicious Rhubarb Smoothie! This smoothie only takes a few minutes to prep and is loaded with fresh and healthy Ingredients.
Serving: 1
Preparation time: 5 minutes
Ready time: 5 minutes

Ingredients:
- 1/2 cup diced rhubarb
- 1/2 cup fresh or frozen pineapple chunks
- 1/2 cup fresh or frozen strawberries
- 1 banana
- 2 cups coconut water

Instructions:
1. Peel and dice the banana and add it to a blender.
2. Add the diced rhubarb, pineapple chunks, strawberries and coconut water to the blender and blend until smooth.
3. Pour the smoothie into a glass and enjoy right away!

Nutrition information: Calories: 230, Fat: 0.5g, Saturated Fat: 0g, Carbohydrates: 52g, Fiber: 6g, Protein: 4g, Sodium: 40mg, Potassium: 1000mg.

20. Rhubarb Juice

This refreshing Rhubarb Juice is made with real rhubarb and is a wonderful way to cool off on a warm day.
Serving: Makes 8 servings
Preparation Time: 10 minutes
Ready Time: 10 minutes

Ingredients:
- 2 cups fresh rhubarb, cut into 1/2-inch pieces
- 1/4 cup granulated sugar
- 2 1/2 cups water
- 3 tablespoons freshly squeezed lemon juice

Instructions:
1. In a small saucepan over medium-high heat, combine rhubarb and sugar.
2. Cook, stirring occasionally, until rhubarb breaks down and is completely softened, about 8 minutes.
3. Place softened rhubarb in a blender and add 1 cup of the water. Blend until smooth, about 1 minute.
4. Pour rhubarb mixture into a large pitcher and stir in remaining 1 1/2 cups of water, lemon juice, and sugar.
5. Stir to combine and then strain juice through a fine-mesh strainer into a pitcher.
6. Serve over ice and enjoy.

Nutrition information: per serving (1/2 cup): 40 calories, 0g fat, 10g carbohydrates, 0g protein

21. Rhubarb Cocktail

This Rhubarb Cocktail is a delicious and refreshing mix of tart rhubarb and sweet tonic. It's perfect for any occasion.
Serving: Serves 2
Preparation time: 5 minutes
Ready time: 5 minutes

Ingredients:
- 2 cups rhubarb, diced
- 4 tablespoons sugar
- 1/4 teaspoon ground ginger
- 2 cups tonic water

Instructions:
1. In a medium saucepan, combine rhubarb, sugar, and ground ginger. Cook over medium heat until rhubarb has softened and sugar has dissolved, about 5 minutes.
2. Divide rhubarb mixture into 2 glasses.
3. Fill each glass with 1 cup tonic water.
4. Stir and serve.

Nutrition information: Calories: 96, Fat: 0g, Sodium: 28mg, Carbohydrates: 25g, Fiber: 2g, Protein: 0g

22. Rhubarb Lemonade

This delicious and refreshing Rhubarb Lemonade is a great summertime treat!
Serving: 4 cups
Preparation time: 10 minutes
Ready time: 20 minutes

Ingredients:
- 2 cups chopped rhubarb
- 2 tablespoons honey
- 4 cups cold water
- Juice of 1 lemon

Instructions:

1. In a saucepan, add the rhubarb, honey, and 1 cup of water.
2. Bring to a simmer and cook for 10 minutes, stirring occasionally.
3. Strain through a fine-mesh sieve and discard the rhubarb solids.
4. Add the remaining 3 cups of water, the lemon juice, and the rhubarb syrup to a pitcher.
5. Stir to combine and serve over ice.

Nutrition information: Calories 52, Fat 0.1g, Saturated fat 0g, Carbohydrates 12.2g, Sugar 8.9g, Protein 0.3g, Sodium 5.1mg.

23. Rhubarb Punch

Rhubarb Punch is a refreshing summer beverage that's a great way to cool off on a hot day.
Serving: Makes 8-10 servings
Preparation time: 10 minutes
Ready time: 1 hour

Ingredients:
- 8 cups water
- 2.5 cup freshly squeezed lemon juice
- 4 cups rhubarb juice
- 1 cup sugar

Instructions:
1. In a large bowl, mix together water, lemon juice, rhubarb juice, and sugar until the sugar has completely dissolved.
2. Pour mixture into a large pitcher and refrigerate until cold, about 1 hour.
3. Serve cooled Rhubarb Punch in glasses over ice and garnish with lemon slices.

Nutrition information: Each serving contains approximately 57 calories, 0.1g fat, 14.2g carbohydrates, and 0.4g protein.

24. Rhubarb Mojito

Enjoy a zesty twist on the classic mojito with Rhubarb Mojito!
Serving: 1
Preparation time: 5 minutes
Ready time: 5 minutes

Ingredients:
- 2 shots of light Rum
- 1/3 cup of Rhubarb puree
- 2 tsp of light brown sugar
- 3 tbsp of fresh lime juice
- 1/2 tsp of chopped fresh mint leaves
- 3-4 ice cubes
- Club soda (to top off)

Instructions:
1. In a shaker, muddle the brown sugar, rhubarb puree, lime juice, and fresh mint leaves together.
2. Add ice cubes and rum to the shaker.
3. Shake the contents of the shaker until Ingredients are thoroughly combined.
4. Fill a glass with ice cubes and pour in the contents of the shaker.
5. Top off with the club soda and stir.
6. Garnish the drink with a lime wedge and some fresh mint leaves.

Nutrition information (per Serving):
Calories: 150 kcal
Carbohydrates: 22.3 g
Protein: 0.4 g
Fat: 0.1 g

25. Rhubarb Margarita

Drawing from the tartness of rhubarb, this Margarita recipe is a wonderfully fresh and flavorful cocktail.
Serving: 2
Preparation time: 15 minutes
Ready time: 15 minutes

Ingredients:
- 2 ounces Rhubarb Simple Syrup
- 1 ounce freshly squeezed lime juice
- 2 ounces orange liqueur
- 4 ounces silver tequila
- 1 grapefruit wedge, for garnish

Instructions:
1. To make the rhubarb simple syrup, combine 1 cup of sugar, 1 cup of water, and 4-5 pieces of stemmed rhubarb in a small saucepan, over medium heat. Simmer until the sugar dissolves and the rhubarb is very soft, about 20 minutes.
2. Remove the pan from the heat and let the syrup cool completely. Strain out the solids and discard, then store your syrup in an airtight container in the refrigerator.
3. Pour the chilled simple syrup, lime juice, orange liqueur, and tequila into a shaker filled with ice.
4. Shake vigorously and strain into a glass filled with ice.
5. Garnish with a wedge of grapefruit.

Nutrition information: Calories: 216; Fat: 0g; Sodium: 1mg; Carbs: 8g; Sugar: 8g; Protein: 0g

26. Rhubarb Sangria

Treat yourself with a refreshing glass of Rhubarb Sangria that oozes with flavor and aroma. Perfectly balanced with the tartness of the rhubarb, this sangria is sure to be a hit.
Serving: 4-6
Preparation Time: 5 minutes
Ready Time: 2 hours

Ingredients:
- 4 cups chopped fresh rhubarb (about 1 lb)
- 3 cups sweet white wine such as moscato
- 3/4 cup orange liqueur
- 2 cups sparkling water
- 1/2 cup simple syrup

- 1/4 cup lime juice
- 2 navel oranges, thinly sliced
- Ice, for serving

Instructions:
1. In a large pitcher, combine the rhubarb, white wine, orange liqueur, sparkling water, simple syrup, and lime juice.
2. Stir until combined.
3. Add the oranges to the pitcher and stir.
4. Refrigerate for at least 2 hours for the flavors to meld.
5. When ready to serve, pour over ice and top with extra orange slices if desired.

Nutrition information:
Calories: 175 kcal, Carbohydrates: 22g, Protein: 1g, Fat: 0.3g, Saturated Fat: 0.1g, Sodium: 6mg, Potassium: 179mg, Fiber: 2g, Sugar: 18g, Vitamin A: 145IU, Vitamin C: 12.3mg, Calcium: 66mg, Iron: 0.5mg

27. Rhubarb Spritzer

Rhubarb spritzer is a delicious, refreshing drink packed with sweet and tart flavors.
Serving: 4 glasses
Preparation time: 10 minutes
Ready time: 10 minutes

Ingredients:
- 3 cups diced fresh rhubarb
- Juice of 2 limes
- 1/3 cup honey
- 1 liter sparkling or club soda

Instructions:
1. In a small saucepan, combine the rhubarb, lime juice, and honey. Cook over medium heat for 10 minutes, stirring occasionally, until the rhubarb is softened and the liquid is thick and syrupy.
2. Allow the mixture to cool completely before straining into a large pitcher.

3. Pour the sparkling soda over the cooled mixture and stir to combine.
4. Serve over ice in glasses.

Nutrition information: Per serving:150 calories, 0g fat, 37g carbohydrates, 1g protein.

28. Rhubarb Tea

This Rhubarb Tea recipe is the perfect way to enjoy spring's sweet and tart rhubarb vegetable. Boiled in a mixture of spices and honey, this tea will fill your home with warmth and comfort.
Serving: 4
Preparation time: 10 minutes
Ready time: 15 minutes

Ingredients:
- 4 cups water
- 2 sticks rhubarb, chopped
- 1/2 teaspoon ground ginger
- 1/4 teaspoon ground cardamom
- 2 tablespoons honey

Instructions:
1. Bring the water to a boil in a large saucepan over medium-high heat.
2. Add the rhubarb and spices and reduce the heat to low. Simmer for 10 minutes.
3. Turn off the heat and let the mixture cool.
4. Add honey to the tea and strain into individual mugs. Serve warm and enjoy!

Nutrition information: Per serving: Cal 130, Fat 0g, Carb 34g, Protein 1g, Sodium 8mg, Fiber 3g.

29. Rhubarb Coffee

Rhubarb Coffee is a delicious and unique beverage made with rhubarb and coffee. It is simple to make and is great to enjoy on a cozy afternoon.
Serving: 4
Preparation Time: 10 minutes
Ready Time: 15 minutes

Ingredients:
- 2 cups fresh rhubarb, chopped into small cubes
- 1/2 cup white sugar
- 1 tsp cinnamon
- 4 cups brewed coffee
- 2 cups half and half cream

Instructions:
1. In a large saucepan, bring the rhubarb, white sugar, and cinnamon to a boil over medium heat, stirring occasionally.
2. Simmer for about 10 minutes until the rhubarb is soft and the liquid has thickened. Stir in the brewed coffee.
3. Divide the mixture among four mugs and top each with 1/2 cup of the half and half cream.

Nutrition information: Per serving: Calories 155, Fat 10.7g, Saturated fat 6.2g, Carbohydrate 13.08g, Fiber 0.7g, Protein 0.8g, Sodium 27.4mg.

30. Rhubarb Hot Chocolate

Enjoy a unique and delicious take on classic hot chocolate with this Rhubarb Hot Chocolate recipe.
Serving: Serves 4
Preparation time: 5 minutes
Ready time: 20 minutes

Ingredients:
- 2 cups of chopped fresh rhubarb
- 2 cups of whole milk
- 1/4 cup of packed light brown sugar

- 1/2 teaspoon of ground cinnamon
- 1/4 teaspoon of ground nutmeg
- 1/4 teaspoon of ground ginger
- 2 tablespoons of cocoa powder
- 2 tablespoons of cornstarch
- 2 tablespoons of unsalted butter
- 1 teaspoon of vanilla extract
- Pinch of salt

Instructions:
1. In a small saucepan, add rhubarb, milk, brown sugar, cinnamon, nutmeg, ginger, and cocoa powder.
2. Place over medium-high heat and bring to a boil, stirring occasionally.
3. In a small bowl, mix together cornstarch and 1 tablespoon of cold water, then add to the boiling mixture.
4. Reduce heat to low and simmer for 10 minutes, stirring occasionally.
5. Remove from heat and stir in butter and vanilla extract.
6. Divide among 4 mugs. Top with a pinch of salt and additional cinnamon. Serve warm.

Nutrition information:
Per Serving: 145 calories, 8g fat, 15g carbohydrates, 2g protein

31. Rhubarb Pancakes

Enjoy the delicious flavors of Rhubarb in these easy and fluffy pancakes.
Serving: 8
Preparation time: 15 minutes
Ready time: 20 minutes

Ingredients:
- 2 cups All-purpose flour
- 2 teaspoons Baking powder
- 1/4 teaspoon Salt
- 1 cup Milk
- 2 Eggs
- 3 tablespoons White sugar
- 4 tablespoons Butter (melted)

- 1 cup Rhubarb (chopped)

Instructions:
1. In a large bowl, whisk together the flour, baking powder, and salt.
2. In a separate bowl, mix together milk, eggs, sugar and melted butter.
3. Pour wet Ingredients into the dry Ingredients and mix until just combined.
4. Gently fold in the rhubarb.
5. Heat a lightly greased griddle or pan over medium heat.
6. Drop batter into batter onto heat, and cook until golden brown on both sides.
7. Serve warm and enjoy!

Nutrition information:
Calories: 183 kcal
Carbohydrates: 28 g
Protein: 5 g
Fat: 6 g
Cholesterol: 40 mg
Sodium: 167 mg
Sugar: 10 g

32. Rhubarb Waffles

Rhubarb waffles are a delicious combination of sweet and tangy flavors that come together to create a light and tasty breakfast.
Serving: 4
Preparation time: 10 minutes
Ready time: 25 minutes

Ingredients:
 2 cups flour, 2 tsp baking powder, 1 tsp salt, 1 1/2 cup milk, 2 eggs, 2 tsp sugar, 1/4 cup melted butter, 1 1/2 cups diced rhubarb

Instructions:
1. Preheat waffle iron.
2. In a large bowl whisk together flour, baking powder and salt.
3. In a separate bowl whisk together milk, eggs and sugar.

4. Pour wet Ingredients into dry Ingredients and whisk to combine.
5. Add butter and rhubarb to mixture and stir until combined.
6. Grease your iron if needed.
7. Ladle waffle batter onto the iron and cook until golden brown.
8. Serve with butter and syrup or toppings of your choice.

Nutrition information: Calories: 306, Fat: 12g, Saturated fat: 7g, Cholesterol: 86mg, Sodium: 594mg, Carbohydrates: 41g, Fiber: 2g, Sugars: 8g, Protein: 8g

33. Rhubarb French Toast

Rhubarb French Toast is a delicious and easy breakfast. Sweet and tart rhubarb is combined with crisp French toast make this flavorful breakfast dish.
Serving: 4
Preparation Time: 15 minutes
Ready Time: 30 minutes

Ingredients:
- 8 slices of white bread
- 4 stalks of rhubarb, chopped
- 1/4 cup of butter
- 1/2 cup of brown sugar
- 2 large eggs
- 1 teaspoon of cinnamon
- 1 Cup of orange juice
- 1/2 cup of honey
- 1/2 cup of heavy cream

Instructions:
1. In a medium sized bowl, whisk together eggs, orange juice, honey, and heavy cream.
2. Dip each piece of bread into the egg mixture.
3. Melt butter in a large skillet over medium-high heat.
4. Arrange dipped bread slices in the skillet. Cook for 4-5 minutes on each side, or until golden brown.

5. In a medium size bowl, combine chopped rhubarb, brown sugar, and cinnamon.
6. Spread rhubarb mixture evenly over each french toast. Cook for another 4-5 minutes on each side, or until golden brown.
7. Serve warm with a side of honey or maple syrup.

Nutrition information:
Calories: 273, Total Fat: 12g, Saturated Fat: 7g, Cholesterol: 85mg, Sodium: 219mg, Total Carbohydrates: 34g, Dietary Fiber: 1g, Sugars: 17g, Protein: 6g

34. Rhubarb Omelette

Rhubarb Omelette is a simple and delicious dish that combines the sweetness of cooked rhubarb with egg for a breakfast that is both savory and a subtly sweet.
Serving: 2
Preparation Time: 5 minutes
Ready Time: 15 minutes

Ingredients:
2 large eggs
2 tablespoons butter
2 tablespoons diced cooked rhubarb
1 tablespoon of diced onion
Salt and pepper, to taste

Instructions:
1. In a medium bowl, beat the eggs together until they become light and fluffy.
2. Heat the butter in a large non-stick skillet over medium heat. Add the diced onion and cook until soft and translucent.
3. Add the rhubarb and cook for a few minutes until heated through.
4. Pour the egg mixture into the skillet and season with salt and pepper.
5. Cook until the eggs are set, flipping once. Serve while warm.

Nutrition information: Each serving of Rhubarb Omelette contains 134 calories, 9.7g of fat, 6.2g of carbohydrates, 1.2g of fiber, and 7.3g of protein.

35. Rhubarb Quiche

Rhubarb Quiche is an easy-to-make savory tart with a bottom crust, a creamy custard filling and tangy rhubarb topping.
Serving: 8
Preparation Time: 20 minutes
Ready Time: 45 minutes

Ingredients:
- 2 cups rolled oats
- 1/3 cup all-purpose flour
- Sea salt and freshly ground black pepper
- 6 tablespoons of butter
- 1 large onion, finely chopped
- 2 cloves garlic, minced
- 4 cups of diced rhubarb stalks
- 1 cup of cream
- 2 eggs lightly beaten
- ½ cup of grated Parmesan cheese

Instructions:
1. Preheat oven to 375°F/190°C.
2. In a small bowl, combine oats, flour, a pinch of sea salt, and pepper. Cut in butter until the mixture resembles coarse crumbs and set aside.
3. Sauté the onion and garlic in a large skillet over medium heat until soft and lightly browned.
4. Add the rhubarb and continue to cook until softened, about 5 minutes.
5. Grease a 9-inch/23cm deep-dish pie plate and spread the oat mixture evenly in the bottom and up the sides, creating a crust.
6. Pour the rhubarb mixture over the crust and spread evenly.
7. In a small bowl, combine the cream, eggs, and parmesan cheese.
8. Pour this mixture over the rhubarb and spread evenly.

9. Bake in preheated oven for 25-30 minutes, or until the tart is golden brown.

Nutrition information:
Calories: 200 | Carbs: 16g | Fat: 11g | Protein: 7g | Sodium: 142mg | Potassium: 257mg | Fiber: 2g

36. Rhubarb Frittata

This Rhubarb Frittata is a simple yet tasty breakfast or brunch recipe that is sure to become a family favorite.
Serving: Serves 8
Preparation time: 10 minutes
Ready time: 55 minutes

Ingredients:
- 12 ounces rhubarb, chopped
- 1 teaspoon olive oil
- 2 cloves garlic, minced
- 5 egg whites
- 2 eggs
- 0.25 teaspoon dried thyme
- 0.25 teaspoon salt
- 0.25 teaspoon pepper
- 0.5 cup feta cheese, crumbled

Instructions:
1. Preheat oven to 375°F.
2. Heat olive oil in a large skillet over medium-high heat. Add rhubarb and garlic to the skillet and cook until rhubarb is tender, about 5 minutes.
3. In a large bowl, whisk together egg whites and eggs.
4. Stir in cooked rhubarb and garlic to the egg mixture and mix until evenly combined.
5. Add dried thyme, salt, and pepper to the skillet and stir until combined.
6. Pour egg mixture into an 8-inch non-stick baking dish and sprinkle with feta cheese.

7. Bake for 40 minutes or until a knife inserted into the center comes out clean. Serve warm.

Nutrition information: Per serving: 159 Calories, 6g Fat, 8g Protein, 13g Carbohydrate, 2g Dietary Fiber, 111mg Sodium.

37. Rhubarb Stir Fry

Rhubarb Stir Fry is a delicious and quick dish that packs a crunch. It's simple to make and full of flavour with the combination of fresh rhubarb and other vegetables.
Serving: 4
Preparation time: 10 minutes
Ready time: 20 minutes

Ingredients:
- 2 stalks of rhubarb, thinly sliced
- 1/2 onion, chopped
- 1/2 cup of mushrooms, sliced
- 1/2 cup of snap peas, sliced
- 1 tablespoon of olive oil
- 2 teaspoons of garlic, minced
- Salt and pepper to taste

Instructions:
1. Heat the olive oil in a large skillet over medium heat.
2. Add the onions and cook until softened, about 5 minutes.
3. Add the garlic, mushrooms, snap peas, and rhubarb and cook, stirring often, for 5 minutes.
4. Season with salt and pepper and cook until vegetables are tender, about 5 minutes.

Nutrition information (per serving):
Calories: 98, Total Fat: 4g, Saturated Fat: 0g, Cholesterol: 0mg, Sodium: 83mg, Carbohydrates: 13g, Fiber: 3g, Sugar: 7g, Protein: 3g.

38. Rhubarb Curry

This Rhubarb Curry is a unique, sweet and savory dish that combines tangy rhubarb with spices and coconut cream for a delicious meal.
Serving: Serves 4
Preparation time: 15 minutes
Ready time: 45 minutes

Ingredients:
- 3 tablespoons vegetable oil
- 1 tablespoon coriander powder
- 1 tablespoon cumin powder
- 1 teaspoon ground cinnamon
- 1/2 teaspoon ground cardamom
- 1 large yellow onion, finely diced
- 2 cloves garlic, minced
- 1-inch piece of fresh ginger, minced
- 4 cups diced rhubarb, divided
- 2 tablespoons tomato paste
- 1 cup coconut cream
- 2 tablespoons rice vinegar
- Salt and pepper, to taste

Instructions:
1. Heat the oil in a large pot over medium heat. Add the coriander, cumin, cinnamon, and cardamom. Toast for 2 minutes, stirring until fragrant.
2. Add the onion, garlic, and ginger. Cook, stirring until the onion has softened and lightly browned, about 4-5 minutes.
3. Add 2 cups of the diced rhubarb to the pot. Cook for 2 minutes, stirring occasionally.
4. Add the tomato paste and coconut cream and stir to combine.
5. Add the remaining rhubarb and the rice vinegar. Simmer for 20-30 minutes, stirring occasionally, until the rhubarb is tender and the sauce has thickened.
6. Add salt and pepper to taste, and serve hot.

Nutrition information
Calories: 274, Fat: 19g, Carbohydrates: 22g, Protein: 5g, Fiber: 4g, Sodium: 10mg

39. Rhubarb Soup

Rhubarb Soup is a delicious and unique soup filled with tangy flavors. The bright red color comes from the rhubarb that's simmered in a flavorful broth.

Serving: 4
Preparation Time: 10 minutes
Ready Time: 25 minutes

Ingredients:
- 2 tablespoons butter
- 1 large onion, diced
- 4 ribs of rhubarb, ends trimmed, diced
- 4 cups vegetable broth
- 2 tablespoons apple cider vinegar
- 2 tablespoons brown sugar

Instructions:
1. In a pot over medium heat, melt the butter.
2. When melted, add the diced onion and sauté until tender and translucent, about 5 minutes.
3. Add the diced rhubarb to the onions and cook for an additional 5 minutes.
4. Pour in the vegetable broth and bring to a simmer over medium-high heat.
5. Reduce the heat to low and add the apple cider vinegar, brown sugar and salt to taste. Simmer for 10 minutes until the rhubarb is very soft.
6. Let the soup cool, then transfer to a blender and blend until smooth.
7. Serve warm or chilled with freshly chopped parsley, if desired.

Nutrition information:
Calories: 88 kcal, Carbohydrates: 14 g, Protein: 2 g, Fat: 4 g, Saturated Fat: 2 g, Cholesterol: 8 mg, Sodium: 697 mg, Potassium: 319 mg, Fiber: 2 g, Sugar: 8 g, Vitamin A: 275 IU, Vitamin C: 9.8 mg, Calcium: 85 mg, Iron: 0.9 mg

40. Rhubarb Stew

Rhubarb Stew is a tangy and comforting dish with a sweet and sour taste.
Serving: 4
Preparation Time: 15 minutes
Ready Time: 40 minutes

Ingredients:
- 2 tablespoons of olive oil
- 1 onion, diced
- 1 garlic clove, crushed
- 2 stalks of rhubarb, thinly sliced
- 2 tablespoons of brown sugar
- 2 tablespoons of apple cider vinegar
- 2 tablespoons of tomato paste
- 1 teaspoon of dried thyme
- 1/2 teaspoon of ground ginger
- Salt and pepper to taste

Instructions:
1. Heat the olive oil in a large saucepan over medium heat.
2. Add the onion and garlic and cook until the onion is softened.
3. Add the rhubarb slices and cook for 2 minutes.
4. Add the brown sugar, apple cider vinegar, tomato paste, thyme, and ginger and stir to combine.
5. Season with salt and pepper.
6. Simmer for 25-30 minutes until the rhubarb has softened and the sauce has thickened.
7. Serve warm.

Nutrition information:
Calories: 100 kcal, Carbs: 10 g, Protein: 1 g, Fat: 7 g, Sodium: 270 mg, Sugar: 8 g

41. Rhubarb Chili

Rhubarb Chili is a jam-like condiment, combining the tartness of rhubarb with the sweetness of various fruits and spices like cinnamon,

ginger, and clove. This delicious chili adds a complex flavor to any assortment of dishes.
Serving: Makes 2-3 servings
Preparation Time: 10 minutes
Ready Time: 45 minutes

Ingredients:
- 2 stalks of rhubarb, diced
- 1 onion, diced
- 2 cloves of garlic, minced
- 2 cups of diced peaches
- 1/4 teaspoon of cinnamon
- 1/4 teaspoon of ground ginger
- 1/4 teaspoon of ground clove
- 1/2 cup of vegetable oil
- 2 tablespoons of sugar
- Salt to taste

Instructions:
1. In a large saucepan, heat oil over medium heat.
2. Add onion and garlic and sauté for 2 minutes.
3. Add diced rhubarb and peaches. Stir to combine.
4. Add cinnamon, ginger, clove, and sugar. Stir and cook for an additional 10 minutes.
5. Reduce heat to low and simmer for 30 minutes, stirring occasionally.
6. Add salt to taste and remove from heat. Allow chili to cool before serving.

Nutrition information: Per serving: 169 Calories, 7 g Fat, 27 g Carbohydrates, 2 g Protein, 2 g Fiber.

42. Rhubarb Marinade

This Rhubarb Marinade is perfect for adding a sweet and tangy flavor to marinate chicken, pork, or fish.
Serving: 4
Preparation Time: 5 minutes
Ready Time: 1 hour

Ingredients:
- 1 cup Rhubarb syrup or puree
- ¼ cup orange juice
- ¼ cup white vinegar
- 2 tablespoons honey
- 2 tablespoons spicy brown mustard
- 1 tablespoon spicy red pepper flakes
- 1 teaspoon grated ginger

Instructions:
1. In a bowl, whisk together rhubarb syrup, orange juice, white vinegar, honey, mustard, red pepper flakes, and ginger.
2. Place the chicken, pork, or fish in a large resealable bag with the prepared marinade. Seal and shake gently to evenly coat.
3. Place the bag in the refrigerator for at least 1 hour to marinate.
4. Preheat oven to 375°F and cook until cooked through.

Nutrition information:
Serving Size: 100g
Calories: 110 kcal
Protein: 2 g
Fat: 0.9 g
Carbohydrates: 24 g
Sugars: 19 g
Sodium: 135 mg

43. Rhubarb Gravy

This Rhubarb Gravy is a tart and tangy condiment to enjoy with your favorite meat. The sweet-tart flavor combination from the rhubarb and cloves adds a delicious and unique taste.
Serving: Makes 4 servings
Preparation time: 10 minutes
Ready time: 25 minutes

Ingredients:
-3/4 cup diced rhubarb

-3 tablespoons flour
-1 tablespoon butter
-1/2 teaspoon ground cloves
-1/4 teaspoon salt
-1/2 cup water
-1 tablespoon sugar

Instructions:
1. In a medium saucepan, melt butter over medium heat.
2. Add rhubarb, flour, cloves, and salt. Stir until rhubarb is coated.
3. Gradually add water and sugar while stirring until smooth.
4. Continue stirring over medium heat until the gravy thickens, about 15 minutes.

Nutrition information:
Calories: 61, Fat: 2.7 g, Carbohydrates: 9.8 g, Protein: .7 g, Sodium: 106 mg, Sugar: 4.7 g

44. Rhubarb Dressing

This Rhubarb Dressing is an easy and nutritious way to dress up your salads! Featuring creamy feta cheese, tart rhubarb, and a touch of sweetness, this dressing is sure to become a favorite.
Serving: 4
Preparation Time: 5 minutes
Ready Time: 5 minutes

Ingredients:
-2 tablespoons chopped rhubarb
-2 tablespoons extra-virgin olive oil
-1 tablespoons feta cheese crumbles
-1 tablespoons honey

Instructions:
1. In a small bowl combine rhubarb, extra-virgin olive oil, feta cheese crumbles, and honey.
2. Whisk until everything is combined and the dressing is creamy.
3. Drizzle over your favorite salad, or use as a dip for vegetables.

Nutrition information:
Calories: 87kcal, Total Fat: 7g, Saturated Fat: 2g, Trans Fat: 0g, Cholesterol: 5mg, Sodium: 80mg, Total Carbohydrate: 5g, Dietary Fiber: 1g, Sugars: 3g, Protein: 2g

45. Rhubarb Stuffing

This Rhubarb Stuffing is a unique and flavorful way to enjoy rhubarb, perfect for a special side dish.
Serving: 8
Preparation time: 15 minutes
Ready time: 55 minutes

Ingredients:
2 tablespoons butter
1 finely chopped onion
2 finely chopped celery stalks
4 cups cubed bread
1 cup chopped rhubarb
1 cup chicken broth
2 eggs
2 tablespoons chopped fresh sage
Salt and freshly ground black pepper, to taste

Instructions:
1. Preheat oven to 350°F.
2. Melt the butter in a skillet over medium heat. Add the onion and celery and cook until soft and lightly golden, about 8 minutes.
3. Place the bread cubes in a large bowl. Add the onion and celery mixture, rhubarb, chicken broth, eggs, sage, salt, and pepper.
4. Stir until everything is combined.
5. Grease a 2-quart baking dish with butter and spoon the stuffing mixture into the dish.
6. Bake at 350°F for 45 minutes, or until golden and cooked through.

Nutrition information: Per serving (1/8th of total recipe): 166 calories; 8.5 g fat; 2.5 g saturated fat; 5 g protein; 18 g carbohydrates; 1 g sugar; 4 g fiber; 187 mg sodium.

46. Rhubarb Roast

Rhubarb Roast is a sweet and savory dish, perfect for feeding a crowd or a cozy family dinner. It features the tart, tangy flavors of rhubarb in a sweet and delicious sauce served over tender roast.
Serving: 8
Preparation Time: 15 minutes
Ready Time: 1-2 hours

Ingredients:
- 2 lbs. beef roast
- 4 cups fresh rhubarb, diced
- 1 onion, diced
- 1/3 cup brown sugar
- 1/3 cup cider vinegar
- 2 teaspoons cornstarch
- 2 tablespoons cold water
- Salt and pepper

Instructions:
1. Preheat the oven to 350°F. Place the beef roast in a roasting pan.
2. In a medium bowl, mix together the rhubarb, onion, brown sugar, cider vinegar, salt, and pepper. Pour the mixture over the beef, and cover the pan tightly with foil.
3. Bake in the preheated oven for 1 hour, or until the beef reaches an internal temperature of 165°F.
4. Carefully remove the foil and uncover the pan. Stir together the cornstarch and cold water until the mixture is smooth. Add the mixture to the pan and stir into the rhubarb mixture. Return the dish to the oven and bake for an additional 30 minutes.
5. Remove the dish from the oven and let cool before slicing the roast and serving.

Nutrition information: Calories: 432, Fat: 22 g, Saturated fat: 8 g, Carbs: 18 g, Fiber: 3 g, Protein: 33 g, Sodium: 88 mg, Potassium: 680 mg

47. Rhubarb Ribs

Rhubarb Ribs is an easy, tasty dish that combines the tartness of rhubarb with the juicy and savory flavor of pork ribs.
Serving: 4
Preparation time: 25 minutes
Ready time: 1 hour and 15 minutes

Ingredients:
- 2 pounds of pork ribs
- 1 cup of rhubarb jam
- 1 cup of ketchup
- 2 tablespoons of Worcestershire sauce
- 2 tablespoons of honey
- 1 tablespoon of rosemary
- 1 teaspoon of black pepper
- ¼ teaspoon of crushed red pepper

Instructions:
1. Preheat the oven to 375°F.
2. In a small bowl, mix together the rhubarb jam, ketchup, Worcestershire sauce, honey, rosemary, black pepper and crushed red pepper.
3. Place the ribs on a baking sheet.
4. Brush the mixture generously over the ribs.
5. Bake for 1 hour and 15 minutes, or until the ribs are cooked through and the sauce has caramelized.
6. Serve and enjoy!

Nutrition information:
- Calories: 454
- Total Fat: 24g
- Saturated Fat: 9g
- Cholesterol: 128mg

- Sodium: 519mg
- Carbohydrates: 24g
- Fiber: 1g
- Protein: 35g

48. Rhubarb Chicken

Rhubarb Chicken is a flavorful and delicious dish consisting of succulent chicken breasts, rhubarb, and other savory Ingredients. It's a great dish for both weeknight dinners and special parties.
Serving: 4-6
Preparation Time: 10 minutes
Ready Time: 45 minutes

Ingredients:
-4 boneless and skinless chicken breasts
-250g of chopped rhubarb
-1/4 teaspoon of smoked paprika
-2 tablespoons of olive oil
-2 onions
-1 garlic clove
-1 teaspoon of sugar
-2 tablespoons of Dijon mustard
-1 tablespoon of white wine vinegar
-1/4 pint of chicken stock
- Salt and pepper

Instructions:
1. Preheat oven to 350°F (175°C).
2. Heat 1 tablespoons of olive oil in a large, shallow oven-proof pan over medium heat and add the onions, garlic and smoked paprika. Cook, stirring occasionally for 5 minutes or until the onions are softened.
3. Add the chopped rhubarb, sugar and 1 tablespoon of oil and cook for a further 5 minutes.
4. Place the chicken breasts on top of the rhubarb mixture then season with salt and pepper.
5. Mix together the mustard and vinegar and pour over the chicken.
6. Pour the chicken stock into the pan and cover with a lid.

7. Transfer to the oven and bake for 25-30 minutes.
8. Serve with rice or mashed potatoes.

Nutrition information: Per Serving (approximate): Calories: 360, Fat: 9g, Carbs: 19g, Protein: 45g

49. Rhubarb Beef

Rhubarb Beef is a savory dish that combines the tartness of rhubarb with beef for a delicious and unique meal.
Serving: 4
Preparation Time: 10 minutes
Ready Time: 40 minutes

Ingredients:
- ¾ pound beef chuck roast, cut into cubes
- 2 tablespoons olive oil
- 2 cloves garlic, minced
- 2 stalks of celery, sliced
- 2 carrots, chopped
- 1 onion, diced
- 1 cup beef stock
- 2 cups rhubarb, diced
- Salt and pepper to taste

Instructions:
1. Heat the olive oil in a large skillet over medium heat.
2. Add the beef cubes and brown them on all sides.
3. Add the garlic, celery, carrots, and onion, and sauté until the vegetables are tender.
4. Add the beef stock and bring to a boil.
5. Add the rhubarb and reduce the heat to low.
6. Simmer for 30 minutes, or until the beef is tender.
7. Season with salt and pepper to taste.

Nutrition information:
Calories: 321 kcal, Carbohydrates: 11 g, Protein: 24 g, Fat: 19 g, Saturated Fat: 5 g, Cholesterol: 75 mg, Sodium: 211 mg, Potassium: 564 mg, Fiber:

2 g, Sugar: 6 g, Vitamin A: 3414 IU, Vitamin C: 8 mg, Calcium: 58 mg, Iron: 2 mg

50. Rhubarb Pork

Rhubarb Pork is an easy-to-prepare dish that features a sweet and sour taste. This dish can be served with rice or quinoa for a complete meal.
Serving: 4-6
Preparation time: 15 minutes
Ready time: 45 minutes

Ingredients:
-2 tablespoons vegetable oil
-2 cloves garlic, minced
-1 ½ pounds pork shoulder, sliced thin
-3 stalks of fresh rhubarb, chopped
-1 tablespoon soy sauce
-2 tablespoons white wine
-2 tablespoons honey
-2 tablespoons Dijon mustard
-1 teaspoon red pepper flakes
-Sea salt and freshly cracked black pepper, to taste

Instructions:
1. Heat oil in a large skillet over medium-high heat.
2. Add garlic and pork and sauté for 5 minutes until pork is browned.
3. Add rhubarb and sauté for an additional 3 minutes.
4. Lower heat to low and add soy sauce, white wine, honey, Dijon mustard, and red pepper flakes.
5. Simmer for 25 minutes, stirring occasionally, until pork is cooked through.
6. Season with salt and freshly cracked black pepper, to taste.
7. Serve with cooked rice or quinoa.

Nutrition information:
Calories: 235 kcal, Carbohydrates: 8g, Protein: 16g, Fat: 15g, Cholesterol: 55mg, Sodium: 394mg, Potassium: 343mg, Fiber: 1g, Sugar: 6g, Vitamin A: 167IU, Vitamin C: 25.1mg, Calcium: 23mg, Iron: 1mg

51. Rhubarb Lamb

Rhubarb Lamb is a unique dish from South Asia that combines the sweetness of rhubarb with the savory flavors of lamb.
Serving: 4
Preparation time: 10 minutes
Ready time: 40 minutes

Ingredients:
1 1/2 pounds lamb shoulder, cut into cubes
2 tablespoons vegetable oil
1 onion, chopped
1 clove garlic, minced
1 teaspoon ground cumin
2 tablespoons freshly grated ginger
1 cup chicken broth
2 cups chopped rhubarb
1/4 cup cider vinegar
2 teaspoons brown sugar
1 teaspoon salt
1/4 teaspoon freshly ground black pepper

Instructions:
1. Heat the oil in a large skillet over medium-high heat.
2. Add the lamb cubes and cook until browned, stirring to brown it evenly.
3. Add the onion and garlic and cook until softened, about 5 minutes.
4. Add the cumin and ginger and stir to combine.
5. Pour in the chicken broth and bring to a boil.
6. Add the rhubarb, cider vinegar, brown sugar, salt, and pepper.
7. Simmer until the rhubarb has softened, about 15 minutes.
8. Serve hot over cooked rice or couscous.

Nutrition information:
Calories – 211
Total fat – 10g
Saturated fat – 3g

Cholesterol – 71mg
Sodium – 486mg
Carbohydrates – 9.4g
Fiber – 2.2g
Sugar – 5.2g
Protein – 18.7g

52. Rhubarb Duck

This recipe for Rhubarb Duck is full of flavor and is a unique way to serve duck. It is a great way to impress your dinner party guests.
Serving: 6
Preparation Time: 15 minutes
Ready Time: 1 hour

Ingredients:
- 2 duck breasts
- 1 teaspoon olive oil
- 1 small onion, minced
- 1 clove garlic, minced
- 2 cups fresh rhubarb, diced
- 1/3 cup balsamic vinegar
- 2 tablespoons brown sugar
- Salt and pepper to taste

Instructions:
1. Preheat a large skillet over medium-high heat.
2. Rub the duck breasts with the olive oil and sprinkle with salt and pepper.
3. Place the duck breasts in the skillet and cook until golden brown. Remove from the skillet and set aside.
4. Reduce the heat to medium and add the onion and garlic. Cook until softened.
5. Add the diced rhubarb and cook for a few minutes.
6. Add the balsamic vinegar, brown sugar, and a pinch of salt and pepper.
7. Simmer for 10 minutes, stirring occasionally.

8. Add the duck breasts back and turn to coat them in the rhubarb sauce. Cover and simmer for 20 minutes.
9. Serve with a side of veggies and a salad.

Nutrition information: per serving (approximately 6 ounces): Calories: 193, Fat: 9g, Saturated Fat: 2g, Cholesterol: 45mg, Sodium: 96mg, Carbohydrates: 17g, Fiber: 2g, Sugar: 10g, Protein: 11g.

53. Rhubarb Fish

Rhubarb Fish is a delicious dish which pairs the sweetness of rhubarb with the earthy flavor of fish. It is sure to please any palate and can be made in just a few easy steps.
Serving: 4
Preparation time: 10 minutes
Ready time: 25 minutes

Ingredients:
- 4 white fish fillets, 6-8oz each
- ½ cup rhubarb, diced
- ¼ cup white onions, diced
- 1 teaspoon garlic, minced
- 1 tablespoon olive oil
- 2 tablespoons freshly squeezed lemon juice
- ½ teaspoon sea salt
- Freshly ground black pepper to taste

Instructions:
1. Preheat oven to 350 degrees F (175 degrees C).
2. Line a baking sheet with aluminum foil and lightly grease.
3. Arrange fillets on the foil.
4. In a small bowl, combine diced rhubarb, onions, garlic, olive oil, lemon juice, salt, and black pepper.
5. Mix until Ingredients are evenly combined.
6. Spread rhubarb mixture evenly over each fillet.
7. Bake in the preheated oven for 20-25 minutes, or until the fish is tender and cooked through.

Nutrition information: Per serving: 302 calories; 12.7 g fat; 22.1 g carbohydrates; 24.1 g protein; 131 mg cholesterol; 365 mg sodium.

54. Rhubarb Shrimp

This Rhubarb Shrimp recipe packs bold yet complementary flavors - a combination of sweet and tangy, sour and salty. It creates an incredible dish that is sure to impress!
Serving: Serves 4
Preparation Time: 15 minutes
Ready Time: 25 minutes

Ingredients:
- 2 large rhubarb stalks, cut into thin slices
- 4 cloves garlic, minced
- 1/4 cup vegetable broth
- 2 tablespoons honey
- 4 large shrimp, peeled and deveined
- 1 teaspoon olive oil
- Salt and ground black pepper, to taste

Instructions:
1. Heat olive oil in a large skillet over medium heat.
2. Add garlic and stir until fragrant.
3. Add shrimp and season with salt and pepper. Cook until shrimp turn pink and are cooked through, stirring occasionally.
4. Add vegetable broth, honey and rhubarb to the skillet. Simmer until rhubarb is tender, about 10 minutes.
5. Serve warm over cooked rice, if desired.

Nutrition information:
Calories: 126kcal, Carbohydrates: 18g, Protein: 6g, Fat: 2.5g, Saturated Fat: 0.3g, Cholesterol: 43mg, Sodium: 214mg, Potassium: 204mg, Fiber: 1.4g, Sugar: 14.4g, Vitamin A: 213IU, Vitamin C: 5.3mg, Calcium: 45mg, Iron: 0.8mg

55. Rhubarb Crab

Rhubarb Crab is an unusual but delicious combination of rhubarb and crab meant to bring out the pleasant sweet-savory flavors of these two Ingredients.
Serving: 4
Preparation Time: 15 minutes
Ready Time: 30 minutes

Ingredients:
- 2 cups of cooked and shelled crab meat
- 2 cups of diced rhubarb
- 1 minced garlic clove
- 2 tablespoons of butter
- 2 tablespoons of fresh lemon juice
- Salt and black pepper to taste

Instructions:
1. Preheat oven to 350 degrees Fahrenheit.
2. In a medium bowl, combine the cooked and shelled crab meat and diced rhubarb. Add the minced garlic clove and mix everything together.
3. Heat a medium skillet over medium heat. Add the butter then swirl it around the pan. Add the crab mixture and cook for 5 minutes, stirring occasionally.
4. Remove the skillet from heat and add the lemon juice. Season with salt and pepper to taste.
5. Transfer the mixture to an oven safe dish and bake for 15-20 minutes or until the top of the mixture is golden brown.

Nutrition information: 175 Calories, 11.5g Fat, 8.5g Carbs, 11g Protein.

56. Rhubarb Salad

This delicious Rhubarb Salad is sweet and tangy and pairs perfectly with all your favorite dishes.
Serving: 3-4
Preparation Time: 10 minutes

Ready Time: 30 minutes

Ingredients:
- 2 cups rhubarb slices
- ½ cup white sugar
- 2 tablespoons white wine vinegar
- 1 tablespoon vegetable oil
- 2 tablespoons chopped fresh mint

Instructions:
1. Preheat the oven to 350 degrees F (175 degrees C).
2. Spread the rhubarb slices in a single layer on a greased baking sheet.
3. Sprinkle with sugar and white wine vinegar. Drizzle with vegetable oil.
4. Bake in preheated oven for 30 minutes, stirring once after 15 minutes.
5. Remove from oven and sprinkle with chopped fresh mint. Serve.

Nutrition information:
Calories: 108; Total Fat: 3g; Cholesterol: 0mg; Sodium: 3mg; Total Carbohydrates: 19.2g; Protein: 1.1g

57. Rhubarb Coleslaw

Rhubarb Coleslaw is a sweet, tart, and crunchy side dish that takes just minutes to prepare. It's perfect for summer barbecues and potlucks!
Serving: 6
Preparation Time: 10 minutes
Ready Time: 10 minutes

Ingredients:
- 2 cups shredded green cabbage
- 1/2 cup diced rhubarb
- 1/4 cup diced red onion
- 1/2 cup mayonnaise
- 2 tablespoons sugar
- 2 tablespoons white wine vinegar

Instructions:
1. In a large bowl, combine the cabbage, rhubarb and red onion.

2. In a small bowl, whisk together the mayonnaise, sugar and vinegar.
3. Pour the mayonnaise mixture over the cabbage mixture and toss to coat.
4. Chill until ready to serve.

Nutrition information:
Calories: 176 kcal, Carbohydrates: 4 g, Protein: 1 g, Fat: 17 g, Saturated Fat: 3 g, Cholesterol: 8 mg, Sodium: 125 mg, Potassium: 48 mg, Fiber: 1 g, Sugar: 3 g, Vitamin A: 36 IU, Vitamin C: 5 mg, Calcium: 16 mg, Iron: 1 mg

58. Rhubarb Potato Salad

This Rhubarb Potato Salad is a unique and flavorful combination of sweet and tangy vegetables. With a light and delicious dressing, it is perfect for a summer evening.
Serving: 6
Preparation Time: 15 minutes
Ready Time: 1 hour

Ingredients:
- 2 cups chopped fresh rhubarb
- 4 cups chopped boiled potatoes
- 1/2 cup chopped onion
- 1/4 cup chopped celery
- 1/2 cup mayonnaise
- 2 tablespoons cider vinegar
- 2 tablespoons sugar
- Salt and pepper to taste

Instructions:
1. In a large bowl, combine the rhubarb, potatoes, onion, and celery.
2. In a small bowl, mix together the mayonnaise, vinegar, sugar, salt, and pepper.
3. Pour the dressing over the rhubarb potato mixture, and gently mix until everything is coated.
4. Cover the bowl and chill for at least 1 hour before serving.

Nutrition information: 275 Calories; 13g Fat; 35g Carbohydrates; 3g Protein.

59. Rhubarb Pasta Salad

This pasta salad combines the tangy flavors of rhubarb with the crunch of toasted almonds for a delicious side dish.
Serving: 6
Preparation time: 10 minutes
Ready time: 1 hour 10 minutes

Ingredients:
- 8 ounces pasta shells
- 3 cups roughly chopped rhubarb
- 2 tablespoons butter
- 2 tablespoons brown sugar
- ⅓ cup almonds, toasted
- 2 tablespoons balsamic vinegar
- 2 tablespoons olive oil
- 2 tablespoons minced fresh parsley
- ½ teaspoon salt

Instructions:
1. Cook the pasta according to package instructions.
2. Meanwhile, melt butter in a large skillet over medium heat.
3. Add the rhubarb and brown sugar, and cook until softened, about 5 minutes.
4. In a large bowl, combine the cooked pasta, rhubarb, almonds, balsamic vinegar, olive oil, parsley, and salt.
5. Chill the pasta for at least an hour before serving.

Nutrition information: Per serving: 209 calories, 10.5g fat, 25.3g carbohydrates, 4.7g protein, 2.2g fiber, 581mg sodium.

60. Rhubarb Quinoa Salad

This simple and delicious Rhubarb Quinoa Salad is an easy side dish that is packed full of flavor and texture. With a mix of quinoa, tart rhubarb, crunchy walnuts, and creamy feta, this veggie-filled salad is both healthy and delicious.

Serving: 4
Preparation Time: 10 minutes
Ready Time: 20 minutes

Ingredients:
- 2 cups cooked quinoa
- 2 cups diced rhubarb
- ½ cup walnuts, roughly chopped
- ½ cup feta cheese, crumbled
- 2 tablespoons white balsamic vinegar
- 1 tablespoon olive oil
- Salt and pepper to taste

Instructions:
1. In a large bowl, combine the cooked quinoa, diced rhubarb, chopped walnuts, and crumbled feta cheese.
2. In a small bowl, whisk together the white balsamic vinegar and olive oil.
3. Pour the dressing over the salad and stir until combined.
4. Add salt and pepper to taste and serve.

Nutrition information:
Calories: 287, Total Fat: 13g, Saturated Fat: 3.4g, Cholesterol: 13mg, Sodium: 213mg, Total Carbohydrate: 32.3g, Dietary Fiber: 4.7g, Sugar: 5.4g, Protein: 9.3g

61. Rhubarb Rice Salad

This refreshing Rhubarb Rice Salad is perfect for summer meals and barbecues. It combines the sweet taste of rhubarb with the savory flavor of rice.

Serving: 6
Preparation Time: 20 minutes
Ready Time: 45 minutes

Ingredients:
- 2 cups cooked white rice
- 1/2 cup chopped fresh rhubarb
- 1/4 cup raisins
- 1/2 cup chopped fresh parsley
- 2 tablespoons sliced almonds
- 2 tablespoons olive oil
- 2 tablespoons white wine vinegar
- 1 tablespoon honey
- Salt and pepper to taste

Instructions:
1. In a medium bowl, combine cooked rice, rhubarb, raisins, parsley and almonds.
2. In a small bowl, whisk together olive oil, vinegar, honey, and salt and pepper.
3. Pour dressing over the rice mixture and stir to combine.
4. Cover and chill in the refrigerator for at least 30 minutes, to allow flavors to combine.

Nutrition information: (Per Serving)
Calories: 169 kcal, Carbohydrates: 16 g, Protein: 2 g, Fat: 9 g, Saturated Fat: 1 g, Sodium: 37 mg, Potassium: 178 mg, Fiber: 2 g, Sugar: 4 g, Vitamin A: 264 IU, Vitamin C: 3 mg, Calcium: 27 mg, Iron: 1 mg

62. Rhubarb Bean Salad

This Rhubarb Bean Salad makes a delicious and healthy side dish to any meal. Filled with protein-packed black beans and sweet rhubarb, this crunchy salad is balanced with a zesty lime and chili dressing.
Serving: 10
Preparation Time: 15 minutes
Ready Time: 15 minutes

Ingredients:
- 3 cups rhubarb, chopped
- 1 can (15 ounces) black beans, drained and rinsed

- 2 cups coconut, shredded
- 1 cup cilantro, chopped
- 2 limes, zested and juiced
- 2 jalapeños, seeded and finely chopped
- 2 cloves garlic, minced
- 1 tablespoon honey
- Salt and pepper, to taste

Instructions:

1. In a large bowl, combine all the Ingredients from the rhubarb to the garlic.
2. Pour in the lime juice and honey and mix until fully combined.
3. Season with salt and pepper and mix again.
4. Refrigerate for 1-2 hours before serving.

Nutrition information:
- Calories: 240
- Protein: 7 g
- Fat: 7 g
- Carbs: 39 g
- Fiber: 7 g

63. Rhubarb Egg Salad

This Rhubarb Egg Salad is a unique spin on a classic dish, featuring tart rhubarb, boiled eggs, celery, and a delicious creamy sauce.
Serving: 4
Preparation time: 15 minutes
Ready time: 15 minutes

Ingredients:

- 6 stalks of rhubarb, chopped
- 4 boiled eggs, diced
- 3 stalks of celery, chopped
- 1/4 cup mayonnaise
- 1 Tbsp honey
- 2 Tbsps Dijon mustard
- 2 Tbsps finely chopped fresh chives

- 1/4 tsp garlic powder
- Salt and pepper to taste

Instructions:
1. In a large bowl, combine the rhubarb, eggs, celery, mayonnaise, honey, mustard, fresh chives, garlic powder, salt, and pepper.
2. Mix all the Ingredients until fully combined.
3. Place the egg salad in the refrigerator for at least 30 minutes to allow the flavors to meld.
4. Serve chilled.

Nutrition information: Per serving, this Rhubarb Egg Salad contains 160 calories, 11.5 g fat, 6 g carbohydrates, 7 g protein, and 2.2 g fiber.

64. Rhubarb Chicken Salad

Rhubarb Chicken Salad is a delicious and refreshing salad for hot summer days. Its tangy sweet-and-sour flavors come from fresh rhubarb, crunchy celery, juicy chicken, and creamy mayonnaise.
Serving: 8 servings
Preparation time: 10 minutes
Ready time: 25 minutes

Ingredients:
- 2 cups diced cooked chicken
- 1 cup diced rhubarb
- 2 stalks celery, diced
- 1/2 cup mayonnaise
- 2 tablespoons fresh parsley, minced
- Salt and pepper

Instructions:
1. In a medium bowl, mix together chicken, rhubarb, celery, parsley, and mayonnaise.
2. Season with salt and pepper to taste.
3. Refrigerate for 15 minutes to allow flavors to combine.
4. Serve chilled.

Nutrition information:
Per serving: 137 calories, 10 g fat, 8 g carbohydrates, 4 g protein, 2 g fiber

65. Rhubarb Tuna Salad

Rhubarb Tuna Salad is an easy, healthy, and delicious meal that's perfect for a light lunch. It utilizes nutty rhubarb as the star Ingredient, giving a unique flavor to the classic tuna salad.
Serving: Makes around 4 servings.
Preparation Time: 10 minutes
Ready Time: 10 minutes

Ingredients:
- 4 cups chopped rhubarb
- 4 cans tuna (in oil or spring water)
- 1/4 cup mayonnaise
- 2 tablespoons chopped onion
- 1 tablespoon lemon juice
- 1 teaspoon sugar
- 2 tablespoons chopped parsley
- Salt and pepper to taste

Instructions:
1. Chop the rhubarb into bite-sized pieces and place it in a large bowl.
2. Open and drain the cans of tuna and add them to the bowl.
3. Add the mayonnaise, chopped onion, lemon juice, sugar, parsley and salt and pepper.
4. Stir everything together until combined.
5. Serve the salad chilled or at room temperature.

Nutrition information:
Calories – 300,
Carbs - 17g,
Fat - 12 g,
Protein – 29 g

66. Rhubarb Fruit Salad

Try this delicious and healthy Rhubarb Fruit Salad featuring diced rhubarb and a variety of fruits!
Serving: Serves 8-10
Preparation Time: 10 minutes
Ready Time: 10 minutes

Ingredients:
- 4 stalks of rhubarb, diced
- 2 large apples, cored and diced
- ½ cup of fresh blueberries
- ½ cup of fresh raspberries
- 2 tablespoons of brown sugar
- 2 tablespoons of orange juice
- 2 tablespoons of honey

Instructions:
1. In a large bowl, combine the diced rhubarb, apples, blueberries, raspberries, and brown sugar.
2. Pour in orange juice and honey and stir everything together.
3. Allow the salad to chill for 10 minutes before serving.

Nutrition information: (Per Serving): Calories: 127, Carbohydrates: 32g, Protein: 1g, Fat: 0g, Sodium: 9mg

67. Rhubarb Cheese Ball

Whether you're hosting a party or just looking for a sweet snack, this delightful rhubarb cheese ball is sure to be a crowd-pleaser. Paired with crackers, fruit slices or pieces of toasted baguette, this delightful cheese ball takes only minutes to prep and is sure to be a hit!
Serving: 8
Preparation Time: 10 minutes
Ready Time: 2 hours

Ingredients:

- 250g cream cheese, softened
- 50g grated cheddar cheese
- 2 tablespoons finely chopped spring onion
- 1 tablespoon finely chopped parsley
- 2 teaspoons finely chopped fresh thyme
- 2 tablespoons finely chopped rhubarb
- 2 tablespoons chopped pistachios
- Crackers (optional)

Instructions:
1. In a large bowl, combine the cream cheese, cheddar cheese, onion, parsley, thyme, and rhubarb. Mix well to combine.
2. With wet hands, shape the mixture into a ball.
3. Roll the ball in the chopped pistachios to coat.
4. Cover the ball with plastic wrap and refrigerate for at least 2 hours before serving.
5. Serve the cheese ball with crackers, fruit slices, or pieces of toasted baguette.

Nutrition information:
- Calories: 128 kcal
- Fat: 10 g
- Saturated fat: 6 g
- Cholesterol: 32 mg
- Sodium: 182 mg
- Potassium: 75 mg
- Carbohydrates: 5 g
- Fiber: 1 g
- Sugar: 2 g
- Protein: 5 g

68. Rhubarb Guacamole

A unique twist on a classic guacamole dish that utilizes a surprisingly tasty combination of rhubarb and spices.
Serving - 4-6
Preparation Time - 10 minutes
Ready Time - 10 minutes

Ingredients:
- 1 Avocado
- 1 Cup Rhubarb, chopped
- 1/2 Lime, juiced
- 1/4 White Onion, diced
- 1/4 Jalapeno, diced
- 2 Cloves Garlic, minced
- 2 Tablespoons Cilantro, chopped
- 1/4 Teaspoon of Salt

Instructions:
1. In a bowl, mash the avocado with a fork.
2. Add the chopped rhubarb, lime juice, onion, jalapeno, garlic, cilantro and salt to the mashed avocado.
3. Mix the Ingredients together until the guacamole is a uniform texture.
4. Serve and enjoy.

Nutrition information - 170 calories, 14 g fat, 8 g carbohydrates, 5 g fiber, 3 g protein.

69. Rhubarb Hummus

Rhubarb Hummus is an unusual yet delicious take on the traditional hummus. Made with cooked rhubarb, chickpeas, garlic, and tahini, this savory Hummus is perfect for snacking, spreading on sandwiches, or serving with vegetables.
Serving: Serves 4
Preparation Time: 10 minutes
Ready Time: 15 minutes

Ingredients:
- 2½ cups cooked rhubarb
- 1 (15 ounce) can chickpeas, drained and rinsed
- 2 cloves garlic
- 2 tablespoons tahini
- 2 tablespoons olive oil
- 1 teaspoon ground cumin

- ½ teaspoon ground coriander
- Juice of 1 lemon
- Salt and pepper, to taste

Instructions:
1. Place the cooked rhubarb, chickpeas, garlic, tahini, olive oil, cumin, coriander, and lemon juice in a food processor and blend until the mixture is smooth.
2. Taste and adjust seasonings as desired.
3. Serve with chips, pita, or crudité.

Nutrition information: Per Serving: 109 Calories; 6g Fat; 6g Carbohydrates; 4g Protein; 4g Fiber.

70. Rhubarb Pesto

This flavorful Rhubarb Pesto is perfect for spreading on toast, as a marinade or adding to your favorite dish. It can be prepared ahead of time or frozen for future use.
Serving: 4
Preparation time: 10 minutes
Ready time: 1 hour

Ingredients:
- 2 cups finely chopped rhubarb
- 2 teaspoons honey
- 1/3 cup olive oil
- 1 teaspoon freshly squeezed lemon juice
- 2 cloves garlic, peeled and minced
- 2 tablespoons finely chopped fresh parsley
- 1 teaspoon sea salt

Instructions:
1. In a small saucepan, combine the rhubarb and honey. Cook over medium heat, stirring occasionally, until the rhubarb breaks down and becomes soft.
2. Pour the rhubarb mixture into a food processor and add the olive oil, lemon juice, garlic, parsley, and sea salt. Blend until smooth.

3. Transfer the pesto to a glass jar or bowl and store in the refrigerator for up to one hour or freeze for up to one month.

Nutrition information:
Calories: 180, Carbohydrates: 5g, Protein: 1g, Fat: 18g, Sodium: 320mg, Sugar: 3g

71. Rhubarb Dip

Rhubarb Dip is a versatile dip that's incredibly easy to make and absolutely delicious. The combination of sweet and tart rhubarb creates an amazing flavor that can be enjoyed on its own or paired with chips, pretzels, bread, and other dippable items!
Serving: Makes approximately 2 cups
Preparation time: 10 minutes
Ready time: 20 minutes

Ingredients:
- 2 stalks of Rhubarb, diced
- ¼ cup of Brown Sugar
- 2 tablespoons of White Sugar
- 2 teaspoons of Ginger, finely grated
- 2 tablespoons of Lemon Juice

Instructions:
1. Preheat oven to 375°F.
2. Spread diced rhubarb onto a baking sheet in a single layer.
3. Sprinkle brown sugar, white sugar, and grated ginger over rhubarb evenly.
4. Bake for 10 minutes.
5. Place rhubarb in a medium bowl, add lemon juice, and mix until fully incorporated.
6. Serve or store in an airtight container in the refrigerator for up to 2-3 days.

Nutrition information:
Calories: 24, Total Fat: 0g, Sodium: 2mg, Carbohydrates: 5g, Fiber: 0g, Protein: 0g

72. Rhubarb Tapenade

Rhubarb Tapenade is a unique and flavorful condiment filled with tart rhubarb and warm spices. This sweet and tart tapenade is a great addition to any meal.
Serving: 5-6
Preparation Time: 10 minutes
Ready Time: 25 minutes

Ingredients:
- 6 large stalks of rhubarb, finely chopped
- 1/2 cup of olive oil
- 2 tablespoons of capers
- 2 cloves of garlic, minced
- 2 teaspoons of freshly chopped basil
- 1 teaspoon of sea salt
- 1/2 teaspoon of freshly ground black pepper

Instructions:
1. Heat oil in a medium-sized skillet over low heat.
2. Add the rhubarb, capers, garlic, basil, salt, and pepper. Cook for about 10 minutes, stirring occasionally, until the rhubarb is soft and beginning to break down.
3. Transfer the mixture to a food processor and blend until smooth.
4. Spoon the tapenade into a bowl and serve.

Nutrition information: Per 1 serving: 90 calories, 7 grams of fat, 4 grams of carbohydrates, 1 gram of protein.

73. Rhubarb Bruschetta

This delicious rhubarb bruschetta combines the tartness of rhubarb and the sweetness of honey to make a unique and flavorful appetizer!
Serving: 6 people
Preparation time: 10 minutes
Ready time: 35 minutes

Ingredients:
- 2 ½ cups diced rhubarb
- 2 tablespoons honey
- 2 tablespoons olive oil
- 2 tablespoons white balsamic vinegar
- 2 cloves garlic, minced
- Salt and pepper to taste
- 1 French baguette, sliced
- 2 tablespoons fresh chives, minced

Instructions:
1. Preheat oven to 350 degrees F
2. In a medium bowl, mix together rhubarb, honey, olive oil, white balsamic vinegar, garlic, salt, and pepper.
3. Place sliced French baguette onto a baking sheet and top each slice with the rhubarb mixture.
4. Bake for 20 minutes.
5. Top each bruschetta with minced chives and serve.

Nutrition information:
Calories: 132; Fat: 2.3g; Carbs: 27.4g; Protein: 2.4g

74. Rhubarb Crostini

Healthy and delicious, this Rhubarb Crostini is a great appetizer or snack. With crunchy toast points, creamy ricotta cheese, crisp rhubarb, and sweet honey, this recipe will be sure to please everyone!
Serving: 6-8
Preparation Time: 10 minutes
Ready Time: 10 minutes

Ingredients:
- 6-8 slices of a baguette
- 2-3 stalks of rhubarb, diced
- 4 ounces of ricotta cheese
- 2 tablespoons of honey
- 2 tablespoons of olive oil

• Salt, to taste

Instructions:
1. Preheat oven to 375 degrees Fahrenheit.
2. Slice the baguette into slanted slices, and brush each side with the olive oil.
3. Place slices onto a baking sheet and bake for 5-7 minutes, until toasted and golden brown.
4. Remove from oven and evenly spread ricotta cheese onto toast points.
5. Place diced rhubarb onto each crostini, sprinkle with salt, and lightly drizzle with honey.
6. Place back in oven for another 5 minutes.
7. Serve.

Nutrition information: (Per serving)
Calories: 156 kcal
Fat: 5.2g
Carbs: 22.8g
Protein: 5.5g
Fiber: 1.3g

75. Rhubarb Pizza

If you're looking for a unique and creative pizza, look no further than this delicious Rhubarb Pizza! The sweetness of the rhubarb pairs perfectly with an herb-infused homemade pizza sauce, all on top of a crunchy homemade pizza dough!
Serving: 4
Preparation Time: 1 hour
Ready Time: 1 hour 30 minutes

Ingredients:
• 1 batch of pizza dough
• 4 stalks of rhubarb, trimmed and diced
• ½ teaspoon of freshly chopped herbs such as thyme, oregano, or rosemary
• 1 tablespoon of sugar
• 1 cup of pizza or tomato sauce

- 2 cups of grated mozzarella cheese
- 1 teaspoon of olive oil, plus more for brushing
- Salt and pepper, to taste

Instructions:
1. Preheat oven to 350 degrees Fahrenheit. Line a baking sheet with parchment paper.
2. Roll out the pizza dough and place it on the prepared baking sheet. Brush with olive oil and set aside.
3. In a medium bowl, combine the rhubarb, herbs, sugar, salt and pepper, and mix until combined.
4. Spread the pizza sauce over the pizza dough, followed by the rhubarb mixture and the mozzarella cheese.
5. Bake for 25-30 minutes, or until the cheese is golden and bubbling.
6. Slice and serve.

Nutrition information:
- Calories: 270 kcal
- Fat: 9.5 g
- Carbs: 32 g
- Protein: 12 g

76. Rhubarb Quesadilla

Rhubarb Quesadilla is a Mexican-style dish that combines rhubarb, cheese, and crunchy tortillas. It's a delicious and flavorful treat perfect for a quick and easy weeknight dinner.
Serving: 4
Preparation Time: 15 minutes
Ready Time: 25 minutes

Ingredients:
- 12-inch flour tortillas
- 1/4 cup butter, melted
- 1/4 cup diced onion
- 1/2 cup diced rhubarb
- 1/2 cup shredded cheddar cheese
- Salt and pepper, to taste

Instructions:
1. Preheat a large skillet over medium heat.
2. Brush the melted butter over one side of each tortilla. Place the buttered-side-down in the skillet and cook until lightly golden brown.
3. Spread the diced onion over each tortilla. Spread the rhubarb over each quesadilla and top with shredded cheese.
4. Fold the quesadillas in half. Cook until golden brown and cheese has melted, about 8 minutes.
5. Remove from skillet and cut into wedges. Serve.

Nutrition information:
Calories: 419, Fat: 20g, Saturated fat: 11g, Carbohydrates: 38g, Sugar: 2g, Sodium: 458mg, Fiber: 3g, Protein: 13g

77. Rhubarb Burrito

Sweet and tart Rhubarb Burritos are an amazing way to spice up your day. Enjoy a unique twist on a traditional burrito with this twist on a classic!
Serving: 8
Preparation time: 10 minutes
Ready time: 30 minutes

Ingredients:
- 8 large flour tortillas
- 1 onion, diced
- 2 red peppers, diced
- 4 stalks rhubarb, sliced
- 2 cloves garlic, minced
- 2 tablespoons oil
- 1/2 teaspoon cayenne pepper
- 1 teaspoon cumin
- 1/2 teaspoon coriander
- 2 tablespoons lime juice
- 1/4 cup cilantro, chopped
- Salt and pepper to taste

Instructions:
1. In a large skillet over medium heat, add the oil, onion, red pepper, garlic, rhubarb, and spices. Cook for 5 minutes, stirring occasionally, until the vegetables are softened.
2. Add the lime juice and cook for another minute.
3. Warm the tortillas in a large skillet or on the stove.
4. Place the vegetable mixture in the middle of each tortilla and top with cilantro. Fold the tortilla to enclose the filling, and place on a foil-lined baking sheet. Bake for 15-20 minutes in a preheated 375F oven.
5. Serve warm with your favorite sides.

Nutrition information: 179 calories, 11.3g fat, 14.7g carbohydrates, 4.4g protein

78. Rhubarb Enchilada

Rhubarb Enchilada is a delicious combination of sweet and savory flavors that make for a unique yet tasty dinner.
Serving: 6
Preparation Time: 15 minutes
Ready Time: 75 minutes

Ingredients:
- 3 cups diced fresh rhubarb
- 1 onion, finely chopped
- 1 red pepper, diced
- 1 jalapeno pepper, seeded and diced
- 2 cups enchilada sauce
- 10 8-inch flour tortillas
- 2 cups shredded queso fresco cheese
- 1 tablespoon olive oil

Instructions:
1. Preheat oven to 350 degrees F.
2. Heat olive oil in a large skillet over medium heat. Add onions and peppers, and sauté for 8 minutes, stirring frequently.
3. Stir in rhubarb and enchilada sauce. Simmer for 5 minutes.
4. Gently warm tortillas in a few drops of oil for 15 seconds on each side.

5. Place a spoonful of the mixture in the center of each tortilla. Sprinkle with cheese. Roll up and place seam side down in a greased 9x13 baking dish.

6. Cover with remaining enchilada sauce and sprinkle with remaining cheese. Bake for 45 minutes or until heated through.

Nutrition information:
Serving size: 1 Enchilada
Calories: 269
Total Fat: 12g
Cholesterol: 25mg
Sodium: 693mg
Total Carbohydrate: 32g
Protein: 9g

79. Rhubarb Taco

This delicious Rhubarb Taco is the perfect balance of tangy and sweet. It's sure to be a hit with even the pickiest of eaters!
Serving: Serves 4
Preparation time: 20 minutes
Ready time: 45 minutes

Ingredients:
- 2 rhubarb stalks, cut into thin strips
- 1 onion, diced
- 1 red bell pepper, diced
- 1 tablespoon olive oil
- 2 cloves garlic, minced
- 1 teaspoon chili powder
- 1 teaspoon ground cumin
- 1/2 teaspoon coriander
- 1/4 teaspoon salt
- 8 small flour tortillas

Instructions:
1. Preheat oven to 350 degrees F.

2. Heat olive oil in a large skillet over medium-high heat. Add rhubarb, onion, bell pepper, garlic, chili powder, cumin, coriander, and salt. Cook, stirring occasionally, until tender, about 5 minutes.
3. Place flour tortillas on a baking sheet. Divide filling among tortillas and wrap up like a burrito. Bake in preheated oven for 20 minutes.

Nutrition information:
Calories: 260 | Fat: 8g | Carbohydrates: 41g | Protein: 6g | Sodium: 410mg.

80. Rhubarb Burger

This tasty Rhubarb Burger is a simple yet delicious twist featuring sweet and tart rhubarb. It's easy to prepare and makes a great dinner treat!
Serving: 4
Preparation Time: 15 minutes
Ready Time: 45 minutes

Ingredients:
- 1/2 cup of chopped rhubarb
- 1 chopped onion
- 1/4 cup shredded cheese
- 2 tablespoons olive oil
- 1 teaspoon garlic powder
- 1/4 teaspoon black pepper
- 1/2 teaspoon dried thyme
- 1/2 cup bread crumbs
- 2 tablespoons ketchup
- 4 hamburger buns

Instructions:
1. Preheat the oven to 375 degrees F.
2. In a skillet, heat the olive oil and cook the onion for 2 minutes. Add in the chopped rhubarb and cook for an additional 5 minutes until softened.
3. Add in the garlic powder, thyme, and black pepper. Stir in the shredded cheese and combine.

4. In a bowl, mix together the bread crumbs, rhubarb mixture from the skillet, and ketchup. Form the mixture into four equal patties.
5. Place the patties onto an oven-safe baking dish and bake in the preheated oven for 25 minutes.
6. Serve the patties on hamburger buns and enjoy!

Nutrition information:
Calories: 415 kcal
Fat: 14 g
Carbohydrates: 44 g
Protein: 19 g
Sodium: 339 mg
Cholesterol: 29 mg

81. Rhubarb Hot Dog

Rhubarb Hot Dog is a delicious and unique combination of sweet and savory flavors. An unlikely pairing of rhubarb and hot dogs, this dish brings together tart and sweet with a hint of spice. The result is a truly unusual and delicious treat.
Serving: 4
Preparation Time: 15 minutes
Ready Time: 15 minutes

Ingredients:
- 4 hot dogs
- 1 cup chopped fresh rhubarb
- 2 tablespoons honey
- 2 tablespoons chopped fresh dill
- 1 tablespoon olive oil
- 1 teaspoon ground cumin
- Salt and pepper to taste

Instructions:
1. Preheat oven to 375°F.
2. Place hot dogs on a baking sheet and bake for 15 minutes, or until heated through.

3. Meanwhile, in a medium bowl, combine rhubarb, honey, dill, olive oil, cumin, salt and pepper and mix until well combined.
4. Transfer hot dogs to a serving plate and top each with a spoonful of the rhubarb mixture.
5. Serve immediately.

Nutrition information: Calories: 240,Fat: 12g,Saturated Fat: 4g,Trans Fat: 0g,Carbohydrates: 18g,Fiber: 2g,Sugar: 11g,Protein: 13g,Sodium: 500mg,Cholesterol: 33mg.

82. Rhubarb Sandwich

This Rhubarb Sandwich is a simple yet delicious dish that is perfect for breakfast, lunch or as a snack. With just a few ingredients it takes minimal effort to prepare and cook.
Serving: Makes 1 sandwich
Preparation Time: 5 minutes
Ready Time: 10 minutes

Ingredients:
-2 slices of your favorite bread
-2 tablespoons cream cheese
-2 tablespoons rhubarb chutney

Instructions:
1. Toast the slices of bread in a toaster or on a skillet.
2. Spread cream cheese over one slice of toast.
3. Spread rhubarb chutney over the other slice of toast.
4. Place the slices of toast together to make a sandwich.
5. Cut the sandwich in half and enjoy!

Nutrition information:
Calories: 350kcal
Carbohydrates: 38g
Protein: 7g
Fat: 17g
Fiber: 4g

83. Rhubarb Wrap

This Rhubarb Wrap is a healthy, light and flavorful lunch choice that is quick and easy to make.
Serving: 2-3
Preparation time: 10 minutes
Ready time: 25 minutes

Ingredients:
- 2-3 large whole-wheat tortillas
- 1 cup diced rhubarb
- 1 tsp olive oil
- 2 tsp maple syrup
- 2 tbsp minced onions
- 1 cup baby spinach
- 1/2 cup crumbled feta cheese
- 1/2 cup diced red peppers

Instructions:
1. Preheat oven to 350°F.
2. Heat oil in a medium skillet over medium-high heat. Add in rhubarb, maple syrup, and minced onion. Cook, stirring occasionally, until rhubarb softens and mixture is fragrant, about 5 minutes. Set aside.
3. Place tortillas on a large baking sheet and spread rhubarb mixture over each tortilla. Top with spinach, feta cheese, and red peppers.
4. Bake in preheated oven until tortillas are golden and lightly crisp, about 25 minutes.
5. Slice each wrap into 4-6 pieces and serve.

Nutrition information: Per serving (2-3): 170 calories, 7g fat, 24g carbohydrates, 6g protein.

84. Rhubarb Panini

Rhubarb Panini combines sweet rhubarb with spicy arugula for a savory flavor and unique texture. This flavorful sandwich is great for lunch, dinner or snack.

Serving: 1
Preparation Time: 10 minutes
Ready Time: 10 minutes

Ingredients:
- 2 slices of whole wheat bread
- 1/4 cup rhubarb, thinly sliced
- 1 tablespoon extra virgin olive oil
- 1/4 cup arugula
- Freshly ground black pepper to taste

Instructions:
1. Heat a large skillet over medium heat.
2. Brush each side of the bread with extra virgin olive oil.
3. Place the bread onto the skillet.
4. Place the rhubarb slices onto one side of the bread and place the arugula onto the other side.
5. Grill the sandwich for 2 -3 minutes until the bread is lightly toasted and the rhubarb and arugula have wilted.
6. Serve warm.

Nutrition information: Per Serving: Calories: 236, Total Fat: 11.7g, Saturated Fat: 1.5g, Cholesterol: 0mg, Sodium: 229mg, Fiber: 4.9g, Carbohydrates: 33g, Protein: 5.3g.

85. Rhubarb Grilled Cheese

This savory-sweet combination of Rhubarb Grilled Cheese is a perfect lunch that you won't be able to get enough of! It features the tang of rhubarb and the richness of cheese in a delicious sandwich.
Serving:
Makes 1 sandwich
Preparation time: 5 minutes
Ready time: 10 minutes

Ingredients:
- 2 slices of whole-grain bread
- 2 ounces of shredded cheese (such as cheddar, Gruyere, or Swiss)

- 2 tablespoons of unsalted butter, melted
- 2 tablespoons of honey
- 1/4 cup of diced fresh or frozen rhubarb
- Salt and pepper, to taste

Instructions:
1. Preheat a skillet or griddle over medium-high heat.
2. In a bowl, mix together the shredded cheese, honey, and rhubarb.
3. Spread the butter onto one side of each slice of bread.
4. Place one slice of bread onto the skillet or griddle, butter-side down.
5. Sprinkle the cheese mixture over the bread.
6. Top with the other slice of bread, butter-side up.
7. Press down lightly to ensure even cooking.
8. Grill for 3-5 minutes, until cheese is melted and the sandwich is golden brown and crispy.
9. Flip and continue cooking until the other side is golden brown and crispy.
10. Serve warm.

Nutrition information:
Calories: 390, Fat: 18g, Carbohydrates: 41g, Protein: 15g, Sodium: 440mg

86. Rhubarb Focaccia

This rustic Rhubarb Focaccia pairs savory and sweet for an amazing yet simple bake.
Serving: 8
Preparation Time: 20 minutes
Ready Time: 1 hour

Ingredients:
- 2/3 cup olive oil
- 2 tablespoons sugar
- 2 tablespoons finely chopped fresh rosemary
- 2 teaspoons sea salt
- 1/2 teaspoon black pepper
- 2 1/2 cups all-purpose flour
- 1 teaspoon active dry yeast

- 2/3 cup warm water
- 1/2 cup fresh rhubarb, chopped

Instructions:
1. In a mixing bowl, combine the olive oil, sugar, rosemary, salt, and pepper. Mix until everything is combined.
2. In a separate bowl, whisk together the flour, yeast, and warm water until a dough forms.
3. Knead the dough for 5 minutes, then cover it with a damp cloth and let it rise for 30 minutes.
4. Preheat the oven to 400 degrees F.
5. On a lightly floured surface, roll out the dough to a 12-inch circle and place it on an ungreased baking sheet.
6. Sprinkle the chopped rhubarb over the dough and then top with the olive oil mixture.
7. Bake for 25 minutes, until the edges of the dough are golden brown and the rhubarb is tender.
8. Let the focaccia cool for 10 minutes before slicing and serving.

Nutrition information:
Serving size: 1/8 of the focaccia
Calories: 286
Fat: 17.2g
Carbohydrates: 28.8g
Protein: 3.7g

87. Rhubarb Bagel

Enhance the taste buds with this delicious combination of rhubarb and bagel. Rhubarb Bagel is topped with cream cheese and raspberry jam for a delicious contrast of flavors and textures.
Serving: 6
Preparation time: 15 minutes
Ready time: 30 minutes

Ingredients:
- 3 cups white bread flour
- 1 teaspoon yeast

- 1 teaspoon salt
- 2 tablespoons sugar
- 1 cup warm milk
- 1/4 cup butter
- 1 cup rhubarb, diced
- 3 tablespoons cream cheese
- 3 tablespoons raspberry jam

Instructions:
1. In a bowl, combine the flour, yeast, salt, and sugar. Add the warm milk and butter and mix until it forms a dough. Knead the dough for a few minutes and then cover with a damp cloth and let it rise for about 15 minutes.
2. After the dough has risen, knead it again and sprinkle the rhubarb onto it. Form the dough into a bagel shape and let it rise another 15 minutes.
3. Preheat your oven to 350°F and bake the bagel for about 20 minutes.
4. Spread the cream cheese and raspberry jam onto the warm bagel and serve.

Nutrition information:Calories: 245, Carbohydrates: 25g, Protein: 6.2g, Fat: 11g, Sodium: 265mg

88. Rhubarb English Muffin

Rhubarb English Muffin is a delicious snack perfect for breakfast or brunch. It has a burst of flavor thanks to the addition of tart rhubarb and sweet pastry . This quick recipe is easy to make and can be enjoyed in no time!
Serving: 8
Preparation Time: 10 minutes
Ready Time: 15 minutes

Ingredients:
- 2 cups all purpose flour
- 2 teaspoons baking powder
- 1/4 teaspoon salt
- 3/4 cup granulated sugar

- 2 tablespoons butter, melted
- 3/4 cup rhubarb, diced
- 2 eggs
- 1/2 cups milk

Instructions:
1. Preheat oven to 375 degrees and prepare muffin tin with paper liners.
2. In a medium bowl, sift together flour, baking powder, and salt.
3. In a separate bowl, whisk together sugar, eggs, butter, and milk.
4. Add dry Ingredients to wet Ingredients and mix until just combined.
5. Add rhubarb and mix until evenly distributed.
6. Pour batter into prepared muffin tins about 3/4 full.
7. Bake for 15 minutes or until golden brown. Allow to cool before serving.

Nutrition information: per serving
- Calories: 200
- Total Fat: 5g
- Saturated Fat: 3g
- Trans Fat: 0g
- Cholesterol: 30mg
- Sodium: 175mg
- Carbohydrates: 36g
- Fiber: 1g
- Sugar: 25g
- Protein: 4g

89. Rhubarb Biscuit

This Rhubarb Biscuit is a quick and delicious variation on the traditional biscuit that is sure to delight both adults and children alike. With its sweet and tart notes, this biscuit is a real crowd pleaser.
Serving: 4
Preparation Time: 10 minutes
Ready Time: 25 minutes

Ingredients:
- 2 cups all-purpose flour

- 1 teaspoon baking powder
- 3 tablespoons sugar
- 1/2 teaspoon salt
- 1 cup butter, melted
- 2 eggs
- 2 cups coarsely chopped rhubarb

Instructions:
1. Preheat oven to 375°F.
2. In a large bowl, whisk together the flour, baking powder, sugar, and salt.
3. Add the melted butter and eggs and mix until well combined.
4. Stir in the rhubarb until evenly distributed.
5. On an ungreased baking sheet, spoon the batter out into 4 equal biscuit shapes.
6. Bake for 20-25 minutes, until golden brown.

Nutrition information: Serving size 1 biscuit – Calories 231, Total fat 15g, Saturated fat 9g, Cholesterol 59mg, Sodium 187mg, Total Carbohydrate 20g, Dietary fiber 1g, Sugars 5g, Protein 3g.

90. Rhubarb Croissant

This Rhubarb Croissant is an easy to make, pastry dessert made with rhubarb in a buttery and flaky croissant shell. It's the perfect way to use fresh rhubarb and goes great with a scoop of ice cream for a delicious end to any meal.
Serving: 4-6
Preparation Time: 10 minutes
Ready Time: 45 minutes

Ingredients:
- 1 sheet of puff pastry
- 2 stalks of rhubarb, chopped
- 3/4 cup granulated sugar
- 2 tablespoons all-purpose flour
- 2 tablespoons butter, melted
- 1 teaspoon vanilla extract

Instructions:
1. Preheat oven to 400 degrees (F).
2. In a medium bowl, combine rhubarb, sugar, and flour and stir to combine.
3. Cut puff pastry into 4-6 pieces.
4. Place rhubarb mixture in the center of each puff pastry piece.
5. Fold the puff pastry up and around the rhubarb filling, pinching the seams together.
6. Place croissants on a parchment lined baking sheet.
7. Bake for 25-30 minutes, or until golden brown.
8. Remove croissants from the oven and brush with the melted butter and sprinkle with the vanilla extract.

Nutrition information: Each serving of Rhubarb Croissant contains approximately 120 calories, 5 grams of fat, 17 grams of carbohydrates, and 1 gram of protein.

91. Rhubarb Danish

This delicious Rhubarb Danish is a perfect addition to brunch, or a great treat to finish off a meal. It's a light and fluffy pastry filled with a sweet-tart rhubarb compote and topped with icing for a delicious dessert.
Serving: Makes 8 pieces.
Preparation time: 10 minutes.
Ready time: 45 minutes

Ingredients:
- 1 cup rhubarb, cut into ½ inch pieces
- 1 cup sugar, divided
- ¼ teaspoon ground ginger
- 1 teaspoon vanilla extract
- 2 tablespoons cornstarch
- 1 sheet puff pastry, thawed
- 2 tablespoons butter
- 2 tablespoons water
- ½ cup icing sugar

Instructions:
1. Preheat oven to 400°F (200°C).
2. In a medium saucepan, bring the rhubarb, ¾ cup sugar, ginger, vanilla and cornstarch to a boil. Simmer for 2–3 minutes until sauce has thickened. Set aside.
3. Line a baking sheet with parchment paper and lay the puff pastry sheet on top. Cut into 8 even pieces.
4. Spoon the rhubarb mixture into the center of each pastry piece, then fold the edges up slightly to enclose the filling.
5. In a small saucepan, melt the butter and water together with the remaining ¼ cup sugar.
6. Brush the pastry pieces with the butter and sugar mixture.
7. Bake for 25 minutes or until the pastry is golden brown.
8. Let cool, then top with icing sugar.

Nutrition information
Per piece: 200 calories; 9 g fat; 28 g carbohydrates; 1 g protein; 0 g fiber.

92. Rhubarb Turnover

The Rhubarb Turnover is a delicious and buttery pastry with a sweet and tart filling. This turnover is perfect for breakfast, brunch or a snack.
Serving: 8
Preparation time: 15 minutes
Ready time: 45 minutes

Ingredients:
- 2 cups diced fresh rhubarb
- ¾ cup granulated sugar
- 2 tablespoons cornstarch
- 2 sheets (1 box) of frozen puff pastry, thawed
- All-purpose flour, for dusting
- 1 egg, beaten

Instructions:
1. Preheat the oven to 350°F (175°C) and line two baking sheets with parchment paper.

2. In a medium bowl, mix together the diced rhubarb, sugar and cornstarch.
3. On a lightly floured surface, roll out each sheet of puff pastry into an 8x8-inch (20x20 cm) square.
4. Cut the puff pastry into quarters and place the rhubarb filling in the center of each.
5. Moisten the edges with the beaten egg and fold over to seal.
6. Place the turnovers on the prepared baking sheets and brush each with the beaten egg.
7. Bake for 20-25 minutes or until golden brown.
8. Serve warm.

Nutrition information: Per Serving : 371 calories; 19.1 g fat; 0.9 g saturated fat; 44.9 g carbohydrates; 3.9 g protein

93. Rhubarb Empanada

Rhubarb Empanada is a delicious pastry dish with sweet and tangy rhubarb filling inside.
Serving: Makes 8 empanadas
Preparation time: 45 minutes
Ready time: 1 hour

Ingredients:
- 2 cups all-purpose flour
- 1 teaspoon salt
- 3/4 cup butter, chilled and diced
- 4 to 5 tablespoons ice cold water
- 2 large eggs
- 1/2 cup white sugar
- 2 tablespoons all-purpose flour
- 1/2 teaspoon ground cinnamon
- 4 cups diced rhubarb

Instructions:
1. Preheat oven to 400 degrees F (200 degrees C).
2. In a medium bowl, combine 2 cups flour and salt. Cut in butter using a pastry blender, and mix until the mixture resembles coarse crumbs.

Gradually add in cold water, and blend with a fork until mixture forms a ball. Cover with plastic wrap, and refrigerate 30 minutes.

3. In a small bowl, beat eggs; stir in sugar, 2 tablespoons flour, and cinnamon; mix until smooth. Gently fold the egg mixture into the rhubarb; set aside.

4. On a lightly floured surface, roll the pastry dough out to 1/8-inch thickness. Cut into 8 circles with a 6-inch round cookie cutter.

5. Place 1/3 cup filling onto the center of each pastry circle. Fold circles in half over filling, and press edges together with fingertips; mark crimped edges with a fork.

6. Place pies on ungreased baking sheets. Bake in preheated oven for approximately 20 minutes, until golden brown.

Nutrition information:
Calories: 312, Fat: 12g, Cholesterol: 54mg, Sodium: 315mg, Carbohydrates: 46g, Sugar: 18g, Protein: 4g.

94. Rhubarb Samosa

An Indian classic, Rhubarb Samosa is a savoury pastry filled with tart rhubarb and spices, such as ginger, onion, and cumin. It is an incredibly tasty snack full of flavour and texture.

Serving: Makes 12 samosas
Preparation time: 15 minutes
Ready time: 30 minutes

Ingredients:
- 2 tablespoons olive oil
- 1 teaspoon minced ginger
- 1 small onion, chopped
- 2 cups chopped rhubarb
- 1 teaspoon cumin
- 2 teaspoons salt
- 2 tablespoons chopped fresh mint
- 1 pastry sheet (or 12 ready-made butter puff pastry shells)

Instructions:
1. Heat the olive oil in a frying pan over medium heat.

2. Add the minced ginger, chopped onion, cumin, and 1 teaspoon of salt to the pan and cook for 3-4 minutes.
3. Add the rhubarb, remaining salt, and chopped mint to the pan and cook for 5-6 minutes or until rhubarb has softened.
4. Preheat the oven to 400°F and prepare a baking tray with parchment paper.
5. Cut the pastry sheet into 12 triangles.
6. Place one tablespoon of rhubarb mixture onto each triangle and fold into a triangle to form a samosa.
7. Place the samosas onto the baking tray and brush with egg wash.
8. Bake for 15 minutes or until golden.
9. Serve the samosas warm with chutney or yoghurt.

Nutrition information:
- Calories: 186
- Total fat: 11.5 g
- Cholesterol: 0 mg
- Sodium: 406.3 mg
- Total carbohydrate: 17.4 g
- Dietary fiber: 1.4 g
- Protein: 2.6 g

95. Rhubarb Dumpling

Rhubarb Dumpling is a classic American spring dessert that's sure to please. This easy-to-prepare dish features buttery shortcake dough filled with sweet rhubarb and topped with a caramelized sugar glaze.
Serving: 6
Preparation time: 15 minutes
Ready time: 45 minutes

Ingredients:
- 2 tablespoons butter
- 1/2 cup white sugar
- 1 pound fresh rhubarb, coarsely chopped
- 2 cups all-purpose flour
- 4 teaspoons baking powder
- 1/2 cup shortening

- 2/3 cup milk
- 1/4 cup white sugar
- 1 teaspoon ground cinnamon

Instructions:
1. Preheat oven to 350 degrees F (175 degrees C). Grease an 8x8 inch baking dish.
2. Melt butter in a large skillet over medium-high heat. Add 1/2 cup sugar and cook until lightly browned and bubbly, about 5 minutes. Add rhubarb and cook until tender, about 10 to 15 minutes. Spread rhubarb mixture evenly in the prepared baking dish.
3. In a medium bowl, combine flour and baking powder. Cut in shortening until mixture resembles coarse meal. Mix in milk until dough forms a ball.
4. On a floured surface, roll out the dough to an 8x8 inch square. Place over rhubarb in baking dish. Sprinkle with 1/4 cup sugar and cinnamon.
5. Bake in preheated oven for 30 to 35 minutes, until golden brown. Allow to cool slightly before serving warm.

Nutrition information: Each serving of Rhubarb Dumpling contains 519 calories, 19.3g fat, 75g carbohydrates, and 10g protein.

96. Rhubarb Pierogi

Rhubarb Pierogi is a unique Eastern European dish that combines sweet-tart rhubarb, fluffy dough, and nutmeg-kissed ricotta cheese for a quick and easy meal that will satisfy any appetite.
Serving: Makes 12 pierogi
Preparation Time: 45 minutes
Ready Time: 90 minutes

Ingredients:
- 2 cups white flour
- ½ teaspoon salt
- 1 egg
- 1 cup warm water
- 2 tablespoons of butter
- 4 cups diced rhubarb

- 4 cups ricotta cheese
- 2 tablespoons sugar
- ½ teaspoon nutmeg

Instructions:
1. In a medium bowl, mix the flour and salt.
2. Make a well in the middle of the flour and add the egg and butter. Stir to combine.
3. Gradually add the warm water and mix until a soft dough forms.
4. Knead the dough until it is smooth. Cover with a damp cloth and let rest for 30 minutes.
5. In a separate bowl, mix together the rhubarb, ricotta cheese, sugar, and nutmeg until combined.
6. Roll the dough out on a lightly floured surface and cut into 12 circles.
7. Put a spoonful of the rhubarb mixture into the center of each circle and fold over. Press the edges to seal.
8. Drop the pierogies into boiling water and cook for 8 minutes.
9. Drain and serve with a side dish or sauce of your choice.

Nutrition information: Serving Size 1 pierogi, Calories 141, Total Fat 8.8g, Saturated Fat 4.4g, Cholesterol 39mg, Sodium 187mg, Total Carbohydrates 12g, Dietary Fiber 0.8g, Sugars 3.0g, Protein 4.2g.

97. Rhubarb Gnocchi

Rhubarb Gnocchi is a delightful and unique take on classic gnocchi. The rhubarb adds a subtle tartness that is sure to please your taste buds!
Serving: 4
Preparation time: 15 min
Ready time: 20 min

Ingredients:
- 2 cups cooked rhubarb, diced
- 1 cup all-purpose flour
- 2 large eggs
- 1 tablespoon sugar
- Salt, to taste

Instructions:
1. In a large bowl, mix together the rhubarb and flour.
2. In a smaller bowl, beat the eggs and sugar until fluffy.
3. Add the egg mixture to the rhubarb/flour mixture and mix until just combined.
4. Add salt, to taste.
5. On a lightly floured surface, knead the mixture until smooth.
6. Roll the dough into small balls, about 1 inch in diameter.
7. Bring a large pot of salted water to a boil.
8. Add the gnocchi to the boiling water and cook for 2-3 minutes, or until they float.
9. Drain the gnocchi and serve warm with your favorite sauce.

Nutrition information: Per Serving: Calories: 183, Fat: 2g, Saturated Fat: 0g, Cholesterol: 63mg, Sodium: 97mg, Carbohydrates: 33g, Fibre: 2g, Sugar: 8g, Protein: 7g

98. Rhubarb Lasagna

Rhubarb Lasagna is a delicious twist on the classic lasagna dish. It is made with layers of delicious rhubarb filling and a creamy ricotta cheesecake spread. This dish is the perfect combination of savory and sweet that is sure to leave everyone wanting more!
Serving: Serves 6
Preparation Time: 40 minutes
Ready Time: 1 hour

Ingredients:
- 2 cups of diced rhubarb
- 8 ounces of ricotta cheese
- 2 tablespoons of coconut sugar
- 2 teaspoons of vanilla extract
- 2 cups of all-purpose flour
- 2 tablespoons of melted butter
- 1 teaspoon of baking powder
- 1/2 teaspoon of sea salt

Instructions:
1. Preheat oven to 375°F.
2. In a medium bowl, whisk together the ricotta cheese, coconut sugar, and vanilla extract until fully combined.
3. In a separate bowl, combine the flour, melted butter, baking powder, and sea salt.
4. Grease an 8x8 baking pan.
5. Place half of the rhubarb in the baking pan in a single layer.
6. Spread the ricotta cheese mixture evenly over the rhubarb.
7. Top with the remaining rhubarb.
8. Sprinkle the flour mixture over the top of the rhubarb.
9. Bake for 40 minutes until the top is golden brown.
10. Let cool for 10 minutes before slicing and serving.

Nutrition information: Calories: 229, Fat: 7.3g, Carbs: 34g, Protein: 8.4g

99. Rhubarb Shepherd's Pie

Enjoy a hearty and healthy shepherd's pie bursting with the delightful and tart flavors of rhubarb.
Serving: Serves 8
Preparation Time: 15 minutes
Ready Time: 40 minutes

Ingredients:
- 2 tablespoons olive oil
- 1 onion, finely chopped
- 2 cloves garlic, finely chopped
- 2 cups diced rhubarb
- 3 tablespoons tomato paste
- Salt and pepper, to taste
- 1/4 cup red wine or white wine
- 2 tablespoons chopped fresh mint
- 2 cups cooked and mashed potatoes
- 2 tablespoons butter
- 1/4 teaspoon garlic powder
- 1/4 teaspoon sweet paprika

Instructions:
1. Preheat the oven to 375°F.
2. In a large skillet, heat the olive oil over medium heat. Add the onion and garlic and cook until fragrant, about 5 minutes.
3. Add the rhubarb, tomato paste, salt, and pepper to the skillet and cook until the rhubarb has softened, about 7 minutes.
4. Add the red or white wine and let cook for about 5 minutes. Add the chopped fresh mint and stir to combine.
5. Place the rhubarb mixture in a 9-inch pie dish.
6. In a separate bowl, mix the mashed potatoes, butter, garlic powder, and paprika until smooth.
7. Spread the mashed potato mixture on top of the rhubarb mixture.
8. Bake in the preheated oven for about 30 minutes, until the potatoes have browned and the rhubarb is softened.

Nutrition information: Per serving: Calories: 148, Total Fat: 5 g, Saturated Fat: 2 g, Cholesterol: 10 mg, Sodium: 43 mg, Carbohydrate: 24 g, Dietary Fiber: 2 g, Sugar: 4 g, Protein: 2 g.

100. Rhubarb Moussaka

This rhythmic Rhubarb Moussaka is a delicious vegetarian dish made with layers of creamy rhubarb custard, cheesy sauce, and buttery mashed potatoes.
Serving: 4
Preparation time: 20 minutes
Ready time: 1 hour

Ingredients:
- 2 large russet potatoes
- 2 tablespoons butter
- 2 cups cooked rhubarb, chopped
- 2 eggs
- 1 cup cream
- 2 tablespoons sugar
- 1 teaspoon vanilla extract
- 2 tablespoons all-purpose flour

Ingredients:
- 1 tablespoon olive oil
- 1 onion, chopped
- 1 red bell pepper, chopped
- 1/4 teaspoon cayenne pepper
- 1/2 teaspoon paprika
- 1 teaspoon ground cumin
- 1 teaspoon ground coriander
- 2 cloves garlic, minced
- 2 cups long grain white rice
- 4 cups vegetable broth
- 1 teaspoon salt
- 1/2 cup rhubarb, diced

Instructions:
1. Heat the oil in a large skillet over medium heat. Once hot add mhe onion, bell pepper, cayenne, paprika, cumin, and coriander. Cook for 5 minutes, stirring occasionally.
2. Add the garlic, rice, vegetable broth, and salt. Bring to a boil, reduce heat to low, and cover the pan. Simmer for 15-20 minutes.
3. Stir in the rhubarb and cook for an additional 5 minutes, until the rhubarb is tender. Serve warm.

Nutrition information: Calories: 365; Fat: 4.7g; Carbohydrates: 69.1g; Protein: 7.3g.

103. Rhubarb Sushi

This Rhubarb Sushi is an easy and fun recipe that will surprise your guests. It combines the tanginess of rhubarb and paired with a miso-like dressing for an unconventional twist of a traditional sushi dish.
Serving: 4 people
Preparation time: 10 minutes
Ready time: 20 minutes

Ingredients:
- 200g of rhubarb diced

- 2 tablespoons of mirin
- 2 tablespoons of agave nectar
- 2 tablespoons of white miso paste
- 4 sheets of nori (seaweed)
- 240g of cooked rice
- 1 tablespoon of black and white sesame seeds

Instructions:
1. Combine the rhubarb, mirin, agave nectar, and white miso paste in a bowl.
2. Place a sheet of nori on a clean surface and spoon 120g of cooked rice onto the nori.
3. Sprinkle with sesame seeds and spread the rhubarb mix over the rice.
4. Roll up the sushi carefully, starting with the edge closest to you and tucking in the sides as you roll up.
5. Slice the roll into pieces and serve.

Nutrition information: Per serving, this Rhubarb Sushi has approximately 210 calories, 5 g fat, 40 g carbohydrates and 3 g protein.

104. Rhubarb Spring Rolls

These sweet and tart Rhubarb Spring Rolls are the perfect addition to any meal. Made with fresh rhubarb, sugar, and spices, these delicious rolls are sure to be a hit!
Serving: 8
Preparation Time: 15 minutes
Ready Time: 45 minutes

Ingredients:
- 2 stalks of rhubarb, diced
- 2 tablespoons of sugar
- 1 teaspoon of ground cinnamon
- 1 teaspoon of ground ginger
- 1/4 teaspoon of ground nutmeg
- 8 spring roll wrappers

Instructions:
1. Preheat oven to 350 degrees F (175 degrees C).
2. In a bowl, mix together rhubarb, sugar, cinnamon, ginger, and nutmeg.
3. Place 1 tablespoon of rhubarb mixture into each spring roll wrapper.
4. Roll up spring roll wrappers, tucking in sides, and place on a greased baking sheet.
5. Bake in preheated oven for 30 minutes, or until golden brown.

Nutrition information:
Serving Size: 1 roll
Calories: 50
Total Fat: 0g
Saturated Fat: 0g
Cholesterol: 0mg
Sodium: 0mg
Total Carbohydrate: 10g
Dietary Fiber: 1g
Sugars: 6g
Protein: 1g

CONCLUSION

The Rhubarb Cookbook is an excellent resource for anyone interested in adding more rhubarb to their culinary repertoire. With an impressive variety of recipes- ranging from traditional favorites to modern creations- this cookbook truly celebrates the unique flavor and versatility of this cherished vegetable. From savory sides to sweet desserts, The Rhubarb Cookbook provides a selection of dishes sure to please every palate.

As a vegetable that is surprisingly easy to grow, rhubarb makes a wonderful addition to any garden. Not only does it add a unique flavor and texture to dishes, but its heart-healthy properties make it a great choice for anyone looking for a nutritious alternative to traditional desserts. From tart compotes to decadent crumbles, this cookbook offers a wealth of delicious ways to include this edible delight in your meal plan.

The Rhubarb Cookbook is a must-have for anyone wanting to explore the world of rhubarb cooking. Providing detailed instructions and tips, as well as helpful notes on techniques and ingredients, this book is a great resource for learning about and cooking with rhubarb. With its simple and straightforward recipes, the book covers everything from simple everyday dishes to elaborate and sophisticated meals.

Whether you are an experienced chef or a novice in the kitchen, this cookbook serves as an invaluable resource for incorporating rhubarb into your cooking. Offering classic favorites as well as inventive creations, The Rhubarb Cookbook provides recipes designed to put a spotlight on this versatile vegetable. From comforting classics to bright and colorful showstoppers, this cookbook is sure to help any home cook create something special.

In conclusion, The Rhubarb Cookbook is an essential guide to those looking to explore the versatile flavors of rhubarb. With its wealth of recipes, ranging from classic favorites to exciting new creations, this cookbook is sure to be a treasured addition to any kitchen. Whether you're a novice or experienced cook, The

Rhubarb Cookbook is sure to help you incorporate this irresistible vegetable into your meal plan. So don't hesitate- pick up this book today and start creating delicious rhubarb delicacies for your loved ones to enjoy!

Printed in Great Britain
by Amazon